Understanding World History

The Renaissance

Understanding
World History

The
Renaissance

Stephen Currie

Bruno Leone
Series Consultant

ReferencePoint
Press®

San Diego, CA

© 2013 ReferencePoint Press, Inc.
Printed in the United States

For more information, contact:
ReferencePoint Press, Inc.
PO Box 27779
San Diego, CA 92198
www.ReferencePointPress.com

LIBRARY OF CONGRESS CATALOGING-IN-PUBLICATION DATA

Currie, Stephen, 1960-
    The Renaissance / by Stephen Currie.
        p. cm. -- (Understanding world history series)
    Includes bibliographical references and index.
    ISBN-13: 978-1-60152-189-7 (hardback)
    ISBN-12: 1-60152-189-8 (hardback)
    1. Renaissance--Juvenile literature. I. Title.
    CB361.C877 2012
    940.2'1--dc23
                                                    2011048993

Contents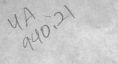

Foreword   6

Important Events of the Renaissance   8

Introduction   10
  The Defining Characteristics of the Renaissance

Chapter One   14
  What Conditions Led to the Renaissance?

Chapter Two   27
  Trade and the Renaissance

Chapter Three   41
  Learning, Science, and Humanism

Chapter Four   54
  Art and the Renaissance

Chapter Five   68
  What Is the Legacy of the Renaissance?

Source Notes   80

Important People of the Renaissance   84

For Further Research   86

Index   88

Picture Credits   95

About the Author   96

Foreword

When the Puritans first emigrated from England to America in 1630, they believed that their journey was blessed by a covenant between themselves and God. By the terms of that covenant they agreed to establish a community in the New World dedicated to what they believed was the true Christian faith. God, in turn, would reward their fidelity by making certain that they and their descendants would always experience his protection and enjoy material prosperity. Moreover, the Lord guaranteed that their land would be seen as a shining beacon—or in their words, a "city upon a hill,"—which the rest of the world would view with admiration and respect. By embracing this notion that God could and would shower his favor and special blessings upon them, the Puritans were adopting the providential philosophy of history—meaning that history is the unfolding of a plan established or guided by a higher intelligence.

The concept of intercession by a divine power is only one of many explanations of the driving forces of world history. Historians and philosophers alike have subscribed to numerous other ideas. For example, the ancient Greeks and Romans argued that history is cyclical. Nations and civilizations, according to these ancients of the Western world, rise and fall in unpredictable cycles; the only certainty is that these cycles will persist throughout an endless future. The German historian Oswald Spengler (1880–1936) echoed the ancients to some degree in his controversial study *The Decline of the West*. Spengler asserted that all civilizations inevitably pass through stages comparable to the life span of a person: childhood, youth, adulthood, old age, and, eventually, death. As the title of his work implies, Western civilization is currently entering its final stage.

Joining those who see purpose and direction in history are thinkers who completely reject the idea of meaning or certainty. Rather, they reason that since there are far too many random and unseen factors at work on the earth, historians would be unwise to endorse historical predictability of any type. Warfare (both nuclear and conventional), plagues, earthquakes, tsunamis, meteor showers, and other catastrophic world-changing events have loomed large throughout history and prehistory. In his essay "A Free Man's Worship," philosopher and mathematician Bertrand Russell (1872–1970) supported this argument, which many refer to as the nihilist or chaos theory of history. According to Russell, history follows no preordained path. Rather, the earth itself and all life on earth resulted from, as Russell describes it, an "accidental collocation of atoms." Based on this premise, he pessimistically concluded that all human achievement will eventually be "buried beneath the debris of a universe in ruins."

Whether history does or does not have an underlying purpose, historians, journalists, and countless others have nonetheless left behind a record of human activity tracing back nearly 6,000 years. From the dawn of the great ancient Near Eastern civilizations of Mesopotamia and Egypt to the modern economic and military behemoths China and the United States, humanity's deeds and misdeeds have been and continue to be monitored and recorded. The distinguished British scholar Arnold Toynbee (1889–1975), in his widely acclaimed 12-volume work entitled *A Study of History,* studied 21 different civilizations that have passed through history's pages. He noted with certainty that others would follow.

In the final analysis, the academic and journalistic worlds mostly regard history as a record and explanation of past events. From a more practical perspective, history represents a sequence of building blocks—cultural, technological, military, and political—ready to be utilized and enhanced or maligned and perverted by the present. What that means is that all societies—whether advanced civilizations or preliterate tribal cultures—leave a legacy for succeeding generations to either embrace or disregard.

Recognizing the richness and fullness of history, the ReferencePoint Press Understanding World History series fosters an evaluation and interpretation of history and its influence on later generations. Each volume in the series approaches its subject chronologically and topically, with specific focus on nations, periods, or pivotal events. Primary and secondary source quotations are included, along with complete source notes and suggestions for further research.

Moreover, the series reflects the truism that the key to understanding the present frequently lies in the past. With that in mind, each series title concludes with a legacy chapter that highlights the bonds between past and present and, more important, demonstrates that world history is a continuum of peoples and ideas, sometimes hidden but there nonetheless, waiting to be discovered by those who choose to look.

Important Events of the Renaissance

410
Rome falls to the Visigoths, ending the dominance of the Roman Empire in western Europe.

1409
University of Leipzig opens in Germany, one of many new universities established during the Renaissance.

1369
Formation of the Hanseatic League, a northern German confederation that valued and encouraged trade.

1452
Birth of scientist, artist, and inventor Leonardo da Vinci in Italy.

400 / 1350 1400 1450

476
The western Roman Empire collapses, bringing the classical period to an end.

1440
Johannes Gutenberg invents movable type, making the printing of books and newspapers easier and cheaper and encouraging the spread of information.

1304
Birth of Petrarch, an Italian who was one of the first important humanist thinkers of the Renaissance.

1345
Petrarch discovers a collection of Cicero's letters; Cicero, a Roman scholar and orator, was an inspiration to Renaissance thinkers.

1466
Birth of Erasmus, a Dutch philosopher who was one of the great humanist thinkers of the later Renaissance.

1514
Polish astronomer Nicolaus Copernicus develops the idea that the earth revolves around the sun, challenging the long-held view that the earth was at the center of the universe.

1503
Leonardo da Vinci paints the Mona Lisa, usually considered among the greatest artworks of the Renaissance.

1517
The Protestant Reformation begins, challenging the supremacy of the established Catholic Church.

1500	1510	1520	1530	1540	/	1640

1522
Erasmus publishes a new edition of the New Testament, allowing more people access to the Bible.

1492
Christopher Columbus reaches the Americas, expanding European knowledge of the outside world.

1512
Michelangelo finishes a series of religious paintings on the Sistine Chapel ceiling, also considered one of the artistic highlights of the era.

1632
Birth of John Locke, an English philosopher influenced by the ideas of Renaissance thinkers.

The Defining Characteristics of the Renaissance

The Renaissance was a period in western European history best known for an emphasis on ideas, commerce, and the arts. It began in the city-states of Italy and gradually worked its way north to Germany, England, and the Netherlands. But although historians agree about what places were affected by the Renaissance, they do not always agree about when the Renaissance took place. Most experts, however, would accept that the Renaissance began sometime during the 1300s and lasted into the mid-1500s. Certainly those years encompass the major events of the era.

The Renaissance was distinctive for a number of reasons. One of these was the degree to which the leaders of the period looked to the past as a model for their own time. They deeply admired the classical era in European history—the years from about 600 BC to AD 300 when first the Greeks and then the Romans had dominated Europe and the Middle East, both politically and intellectually. Many of the most important Renaissance thinkers believed that the classical period was a high point in history. Accordingly, they sought to reshape their own society to more nearly match that of the ancient world. Europeans of the Renaissance, therefore, read classical literature, studied classical philosophy, and valued the activities and ideals that the classical world had valued. Without the example of the Romans and the Greeks to look back on, the Renaissance would never have existed.

The Humanist Perspective

Though the Renaissance had a practical side—it was marked, for example, by a rise in trade, a redefining of what wealth meant, and the beginnings of a technological revolution—the Renaissance was an intellectual movement at heart. It was defined in large part by a philosophy known today as humanism. Humanism is a mindset that values human achievement and celebrates human possibility. At its most basic level, humanism holds that people are individuals, important in their own right and capable of great things. From religion to politics and from art to science, the humanist perspective was present in almost every aspect of the Renaissance—and was a driving force behind many of the changes that took place during the period.

The humanist philosophy appeared in a variety of forms throughout the Renaissance, with each of these forms adding to the distinctiveness

The humanist perspective, which values human achievement and imagination, flowered during the Renaissance and is reflected in Raphael's famous painting, School of Athens. *In this detail from the painting, the renowned Greek mathematician Euclid instructs his students.*

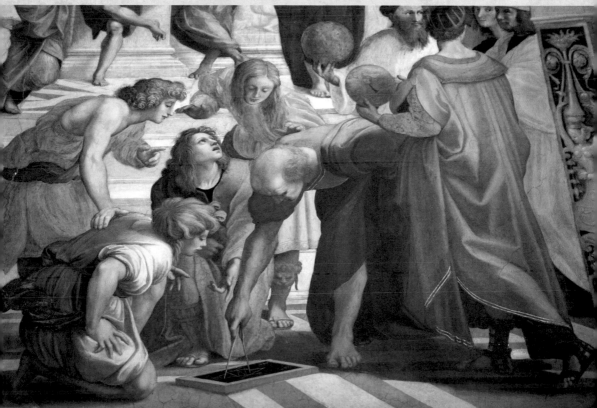

of the period. Perhaps foremost among these was a delight in human imagination. The Renaissance was without question an era of exceptional creativity, especially where the arts were concerned. Italian artists of the Renaissance such as Donatello, Raphael, and Michelangelo created paintings, sculptures, and other works of exquisite beauty and revolutionary design. Further north, artists such as Hans Holbein and Albrecht Dürer of Germany produced impressive artworks as well. And while the Renaissance was best known for the visual arts, the era did produce some important books, notably English author Geoffrey Chaucer's *Canterbury Tales* and German satirist Sebastian Brant's *Ship of Fools*. The humanist leaders of the Renaissance appreciated and lauded this creativity, believing that the ability to create was squarely in the realm of human endeavor and not a talent reserved only for God.

New Ideas and Possibilities

A second feature of the Renaissance was a secular perspective. The word *secular* means "of the world" and is typically used to describe activities that are not specifically religious. Secularism, then, suggests an emphasis on the world here and now, especially in contrast to formal religion, which is often much more concerned with divinities and the nature of the next world than with the issues of this one. Calling the leaders of the Renaissance secularists does not imply that they rejected Christianity, the dominant religion of their time, or that they opposed organized religion. On the contrary, nearly all of the great thinkers of the Renaissance professed a strong Christian faith, and the outstanding artists, writers, and essayists of the period used religious themes and biblical imagery in many of their works. Still, many Renaissance thinkers considered the world from not only the prevailing Christian perspective, but from a less strictly religious one as well.

The humanism of the Renaissance was also reflected in a deep curiosity about the world. Thinkers of the time questioned the assumptions and the conventional wisdom of previous generations. Besides looking back toward classical society, they sought out new knowledge as well—and worked to incorporate that knowledge into their understanding of the world around them. Education, then, was important to the leaders of the Renaissance. So was invention. And although modern scientific thought had not yet made its appearance by the time of the Renaissance, the seeds of scientific reasoning were present in the observations and experiments carried out by Nicolaus Copernicus, Leonardo da Vinci, and others who wondered why the universe acted the way it did—and who were determined to investigate their questions in detail.

The humanist philosophy, an appreciation for the classical period in European history, and advances in areas such as commerce and technology—all of these characteristics helped shape and define the Renaissance. The combination of these features produced a remarkable transformation of European society and culture during the years of the Renaissance. In education and in government, in wealth and in the visual arts, the Renaissance produced major changes in almost every area of European life—changes that even today continue to affect the way people live, work, and think. The Renaissance, then, was an exciting time, a period that seemed full of new ideas and possibilities, and an era that undoubtedly ranks as one of the most compelling of European history.

Chapter 1

What Conditions Led to the Renaissance?

All periods in history are shaped not just by the conditions of their own time, but by at least one earlier era as well. The Renaissance was certainly no exception to this general rule. In two important ways, however, the Renaissance stands out as somewhat unusual among historical periods. For one, the Renaissance was shaped not by one earlier era but two—the classical period of the distant past and the somewhat later medieval era as well. And for another, these two eras, though dissimilar in the extreme, were nonetheless equally crucial in determining the course of the Renaissance.

Ancient Greece

A renaissance is a rebirth—a reclaiming of the ideas, arts, and excitement of an earlier, more glorious time. Even the name *Renaissance*, then, suggests that the people of the era admired the goals and values of a long-gone civilization. That civilization was the culture of the classical period, when first Greece and then Rome dominated the region around the Mediterranean Sea—and sometimes beyond. When the artists, philosophers, and entrepreneurs of the Renaissance looked into the past, they looked back a thousand years and more to these ancient civilizations. Throughout the Renaissance, thinkers and leaders used the Greek and Roman cultures as models and templates for the society they wished to create in their own time.

Of these two great civilizations, the first to arise was Greece. The civilization that the Greeks developed was based partly on trade and technology. Around 750 BC, merchants began building extensive trade networks that allowed goods to flow cheaply and quickly from one part of Greece to another. The growth of commerce increased the Greek sense of unity, raised the standard of living across the empire, and permitted Greek civilization to focus on matters beyond the production of food. As commerce increased, moreover, the ancient Greeks began to develop a variety of devices which made work easier and faster. Greek engineers either introduced or improved on the crossbow, the crane, the watermill, and the winch, each of which allowed the ancient Greeks to accomplish more work with less effort. Together, the growth of trade and technological innovation helped make Greek civilization wealthier and more sophisticated.

In addition to trade and technology, the Greeks are known today for several less practical but equally enduring achievements. Greek artists, for example, produced elaborate works of sculpture, painting, and pottery. As art historians Seán Hemingway and Colette Hemingway put it, ancient Greek art "conveys a vitality of life as well as a sense of permanence, clarity, and harmony."[1] In particular, the Greeks are justly renowned as architects. The best known example of Greek architecture today is a complex of temples, gateways, and other structures known as the Acropolis. The United Nations describes the Acropolis as one of the most important cultural sites in the world, calling it "a complete series of masterpieces."[2]

Perhaps most important of all, ancient Greek civilization strongly valued literature, philosophy, and science. The Greeks of classical times were an intensely curious people, very much at home in the world of ideas. Greek philosophers such as Socrates, Plato, and Aristotle studied and discussed questions of life, society, and government. The poet Homer wrote the epic sagas the *Iliad* and the *Odyssey*, while the playwright Sophocles wrote *Antigone* and other dramas. Greek scientists investigated everything from the night sky to the properties of water. Greek physicians studied the human body in hopes of curing diseases more effectively. Greek mathematicians made important

The literature, philosophy, science, art, and architecture of ancient Greece strongly influenced Renaissance thinkers, artists, and entrepreneurs. The Acropolis (top) is considered an architectural masterpiece of Greek civilization.

geometric discoveries and helped develop the notion of mathematical proof. Biology, ethics, logic—few areas of study were neglected by the ancient Greeks.

The Roman Empire

The military and political powers of Greece began to diminish after about 250 BC, and a new empire became dominant in the Mediterranean region. This was the Roman Empire. Centered in the city of Rome in what is now Italy, the Roman Empire eventually reached from Great

Britain into western Asia. But although the Romans eclipsed Greece politically, the Romans admired Greek civilization and sought to replicate it in their own society. Like the Greeks, for example, the Romans valued commerce and engineering. Roman trade networks stretched across their empire and beyond, bringing goods such as tin, spices, and ivory to Rome from remote places such as Russia, Egypt, and Iran. Many of these trade routes existed only because the Romans constructed hundreds of thousands of miles of durable roads throughout their empire.

Like the Greeks, the Romans were also skilled architects and artists. Roman architecture typically emphasized domes and arches, both of which had been used earlier by the Greeks as well. However, the Romans went beyond the Greeks in their enthusiasm for these features. As one example, the walls of a famous Roman stadium called the Colosseum consisted almost entirely of several rows of arches. Other visual arts likewise drew from Greek ideas but were nonetheless distinctively Roman. Roman sculptors were more likely to fashion busts and statues than their Greek counterparts, for instance, and Roman painters produced many more landscapes than did the painters of ancient Greece.

Finally, the Romans continued the Greek focus on learning and philosophy. Legal scholars wrote and debated laws, eventually creating a comprehensive set of legal principles that lasted, in one form or another, for many centuries. Poets like Horace and Ovid were frequently read and much admired. The orator Cicero was well respected for his insightful ideas on philosophy and government, as well as for the compelling way he expressed them. And though Roman government could be oppressive and unresponsive, Roman leaders did sometimes value the free exchange of ideas. For example, the Roman Forum—a public space near the center of Rome—was used for speech making by friends and foes of the government alike.

The Middle Ages

Like ancient Greek culture, the Roman Empire lasted for many centuries. By AD 200, however, it was beginning to weaken. Around 290 the emperor Diocletian split the empire into two parts, a western part based in Rome and an eastern section based in Constantinople, the present-day city of Istanbul. The eastern sector flourished. The western portion, though, did not. All through the 300s Germanic peoples from northern Europe overran enormous tracts of land belonging to the Roman Empire while the Roman armies steadily retreated. In 410 a Germanic tribe known as the Visigoths invaded Italy and conquered Rome. "The city which had taken the whole world was itself taken,"[3] mourned one loyal Roman. Other outposts of the empire began falling as well. By 476 the western Roman Empire was no more. A new era, called the Middle Ages or the medieval period, had begun.

The people of the Middle Ages took little from Roman culture. Part of the reason was the state of the empire itself. Beset by attacks, revolts, and economic problems, the western Roman Empire of the 400s had little to offer. Moreover, the northern European tribes who overran Rome and destroyed the western empire were very different from the Romans. These Germanic peoples were rough and simple and had little interest in following Roman ways, especially where arts and learning were concerned. The fall of Rome, then, brought major political, economic, and cultural changes to western Europe. "Rising to an extraordinary peak in classical times," writes historian William McNeill, "[Europe] declined in equally extraordinary fashion following the fall of the Roman Empire in the West."[4]

As McNeill's use of the word "declined" indicates, historians have not always been kind to the medieval period. For many years, in fact, the period was known as the Dark Ages—an unflattering reference to the lack of learning and culture during the era. To some extent, this stereotype is an exaggeration. Western Europeans produced a number of important cultural works during the Middle Ages: buildings such as the Gothic cathedrals of France, works by authors like the Italian writer Dante Alighieri. Nonetheless, in comparison with the periods immediately before and afterward, medieval Europe was mostly a cultural backwater. Even Rome, writes historian Steven Runciman, was "a paltry city"[5] during most of this period, overshadowed culturally as well as politically by Constantinople and several cities of the Middle East.

Medieval Maps

Maps are an excellent example of the dim awareness medieval Europeans had about the world around them. During the early Middle Ages, maps commonly showed three landmasses, representing Africa, Asia, and Europe. But geographers of the time had only a vague understanding of Europe's shape and outlines and knew nothing of Africa or Asia except the parts that lay closest to European territory. Africa and Europe were usually depicted as quarter-circles, separated by a narrow line that represented the Mediterranean Sea; in turn, Asia was shown as a somewhat larger half-circle. The maps were useless for navigation, revealed nothing about the distance or direction, and usually showed only a scattering of cities, mountains, or other features.

As the medieval period continued, maps did improve somewhat. Mapmakers made a greater effort to show actual places, often noting them with symbols a lion for Rome, boats to indicate a river, cathedrals to mark religious centers—to make them recognizable and to add to the beauty of their finished work. Cartographers of this time also increasingly tried to depict places in relationship to their actual surroundings. Sometimes they met with at least some success. An English map of the late 1200s shows a reasonably accurate view of the Nile Delta, for example, and other maps of the later Middle Ages show physical features that are recognizable today. Still, the general state of cartography in the medieval period reflected the general lack of knowledge—and interest—in the outside world among the Europeans of the era.

The Feudal System

The medieval period was also characterized by a political and economic system called feudalism. The basic building block of feudalism was land. Through nearly the entire medieval period most European countries were divided into territories known as manors, estates, or fiefs. Each of these manors was under the control of a lord: a prince, duke, knight, or other member of the nobility. The lord of the manor not only ruled the estate where he made his home, he owned it as well. In a sense, the lord owned many of the people who lived on the estate, too. The bulk of a manor's population was made up of peasants known as serfs, who spent most of their time farming. Legally, serfs belonged to the land and could not leave the fief without permission. As historian George Holmes notes, moreover, a serf "could be bought and sold with his descendants . . . and his servile status was inherited by his children."[6]

The food that serfs produced typically belonged to their masters as well. Though serfs were allowed to keep some of the crops they grew, the bulk of what they harvested went to the landowner. Only a small fraction of the crops the serfs raised went to feed their families. Because they were tied to the land, however, the serfs had little recourse if they did not like the way they were treated. Indeed, serfs were required to swear loyalty oaths to their masters, oaths that defined them more as copies of their lords than as living, breathing human beings. "I will to [my lord] be true and faithful," one such oath read, "and love all which he loves and shun all which he shuns. . . . Nor will I ever with will or action, through word or deed, do anything which is unpleasing to him."[7]

Though this arrangement was clearly slanted in favor of the lord who owned the manor, the serfs did receive some benefit from the feudal system. Medieval oaths of loyalty included promises to the serfs as well as promises to the lords. As another section of the loyalty oath mentioned above reads, "It is right that those who offer to us unbroken fidelity should be protected by our [the lord's] aid."[8] Most often this aid consisted of protection should the manor be attacked. Despite this benefit, though, the serfs lived a miserable existence. Their labors were long, their homes small. Many suffered early deaths from overwork, disease, and starvation; historians estimate that the life expectancy of a serf was 30 years.

Consequences of Feudalism

Because the feudal system was at the heart of the medieval world, it had enormous influence on medieval society. Perhaps most obviously, feudalism created a highly rigid and stratified social system. As suggested by the custom that bound not only a serf but also the serf's children

Peasants plant vines and pick grapes under the watchful eyes of their lord. The lives of lords, peasants, and others were dictated by a rigid and stratified social system during the Middle Ages, the period that preceded the Renaissance.

to serve the lord of the manor, there was essentially no mechanism by which a peasant could move upward in society. Once a serf, medieval Europeans believed, always a serf. As for artisans and other skilled workers, who occupied a niche between the peasants and the lords, they, too, were supposed to remain in their assigned station. "A carpenter ought not to try to become a knight,"[9] writes historian Jeffrey Burton Russell, summarizing the predominant view in the Middle Ages.

Another consequence of the feudal system was to narrow the focus of most Europeans. The serfs, for example, did not think of themselves in national terms—as German, say, or French. Neither did they usually see themselves as belonging to a region. Since they were tied to the land, they most often identified solely with their estate and had few allegiances or identifications beyond the manor. That was true even if their fief was part of a larger unit of government, as nearly all were.

To a somewhat lesser extent, the same was true of nobles and artisans. Though England, France, and a few other large countries existed during the medieval period, most of Europe during the Middle Ages consisted of small kingdoms, duchies, city-states, and minor nations. A nobleman from what is now Italy would have been loyal not to Italy—which at the time did not exist as a political unit—but to the region where he lived: Lombardy, say, or Venice, or Salerno. Even in a larger, more stable nation such as England, nobles in the largely Celtic region of Cornwall saw themselves as separate from the nation's Anglo-Saxon and French leaders.

For all levels of medieval society, the effect was the same: Instead of looking for similarities between themselves and their neighbors, the people of the Middle Ages most often looked for differences. Rather than joining together with people who spoke the same language, or finding common cause with those with whom they shared a culture, they kept themselves apart. "Each hamlet was inbred, isolated," writes historian William Manchester, "unaware of the world beyond the most familiar local landmark: a creek, or mill, or tall tree scarred by lightning."[10] Throughout medieval Europe, people were suspicious of those who were not exactly like themselves—of people who lived across the continent, at the other end of a river, or even on the neighboring manor. This perspective made communication among the various peoples of Europe difficult, and it made cooperation almost impossible.

Christianity and the Church

Though Europe in the Middle Ages was fractured politically, it was unified in one important way: religion. While some Jews and Muslims lived in various parts of Europe, the dominant religion in medieval Europe by far was Christianity. The first Christians had been an oppressed minority within the Roman Empire, barred from openly practicing their faith and forced to hold services in secret. During the 300s, however, the situation shifted dramatically as Roman emperors not only lifted the ban on Christianity but also instituted it as the official religion of the empire. Before long, Christian missionaries were spreading north and west into the lands now known as France, Spain, and Britain. By 1000, nearly all the pagan populations of western Europe had become Christian.

The medieval European world, then, was a strongly Christian society in which the Church held great power. Much of this power was spiritual. Religion, after all, offered peasants and nobles alike their only chance at eternal life. Those who followed the path set out by Church leaders might arrive in heaven after their deaths; those who did not could look forward only to the horrors of hell. And horrors they were: As historian Barbara Tuchman describes the common belief of the time, "In Hell, the damned hung by their tongues from trees of fire, the impenitent [people who refused to admit that they had sinned] burned in furnaces, unbelievers smothered in foul-smelling smoke."[11] Medieval Europeans strove to adhere to Church teachings in the hope of saving their souls.

Christianity therefore had an enormous influence on the way people of the Middle Ages behaved and how they thought about the world around them. The Roman Church, for example, taught that life on earth was essentially a test to determine who was good enough to go to heaven. Consequently, medieval Europeans believed that life was

The Church

Through most of the medieval period and into the Renaissance, there were two main forms of Christianity. One, based in Rome, thought of itself simply as "the Church"; it is the direct ancestor of the Roman Catholic faith today. The other, based in Constantinople, called itself the Orthodox Church. Even in the early medieval era it was apparent that there were cultural and doctrinal differences between the two branches of the Church. Culturally, theologically, and geographically, the people of western Europe always looked to the Roman branch of the Church for guidance. When the two churches formally separated in 1054, the western Europeans followed the Church of Rome.

The structure of the Roman Church was strongly hierarchical. Western Europe was divided into individual parishes, each led by a priest or occasionally by a monk. The parishes, in turn, were joined together in a geographic grouping called a diocese. Every diocese was led by an administrator called a bishop. The most powerful of these bishops was the Bishop of Rome, also known as the pope. The pope outranked the other bishops, who in turn gave orders to the priests. The strict lines of authority concentrated power at the top of the Church; the insistence on obedience to superiors, moreover, tended to stifle dissent. Partly for this reason, the Church as an institution was traditionally very slow to change during the medieval and Renaissance periods.

supposed to be difficult, unpleasant, and temporary. Few people saw life as something to be enjoyed. Rather, in the words of a fourteenth-century author, life was "a hard and weary journey toward the eternal home for which we look; or, if we neglect our salvation, an equally pleasureless way to eternal death."[12]

The Church's power was not only spiritual, however. In fact, the Church had as much political power as nearly any medieval king—and a great deal more than many. In the Middle Ages, the Church had the authority to tax peasants and nobles alike, and it used this authority freely, amassing a great deal of wealth in the process. Church officials also influenced the internal affairs of western European governments. Breaking the rules of the Church, in most cases, was equal to breaking the law of the land. A person who ignored the Church's dietary laws by eating meat on a Friday, for example, could be put to death. Moreover, the backing of the Church was necessary for all but the strongest rulers to remain in power. "Kings and princes owed their legitimacy to divine authority,"[13] Manchester notes.

A Stagnant Society

The Church, the feudal system, the reduced artistic achievement, and the focus on local rather than national or Europe-wide concerns—all of these were hallmarks of the Middle Ages. However, the medieval period had other important features as well. It was an exceptionally violent era, for example, when knights killed one another (and commoners as well) at an alarming rate; McNeill writes that medieval Europe was "more thoroughly warlike than [almost] any other civilized society on the globe."[14] Superstition was widespread and almost always trumped reason. Commerce was slow and inefficient, with many trade routes from Greek and Roman times no longer in use. Poverty was everywhere. Famine was a constant worry. And disease—most notably the Black Death, or the bubonic plague, which killed millions of Europeans during the 1300s—was always a concern.

Perhaps the most important hallmark of medieval Europe, though, was not feudalism or famine, not violence or illiteracy, but stagnation. The Middle Ages were a time of slow—and sometimes nonexistent—change. Movement between social classes was almost impossible, and innovation and novelty were rare. New artistic styles were slow to arise and slow to disappear. The Romanesque style in architecture, for example, remained in vogue for about 300 years. "There are great differences between everyday life in 1791 and 1991," points out Manchester, "but there were very few between 791 and 991."[15] Indeed, given the enormous changes in communication, transportation, and information storage in the recent past, it can be argued that nearly as much change has occurred since 1991 as during the entire medieval period.

Medieval Europeans typically accepted the stagnation that marked their society. As a rule, the people of the era were not much interested in investigating the world around them. Few people valued scientific discovery, for example, and fewer still pursued it. Philosophy, political theory, and history were widely ignored. Most Europeans seldom if ever traveled, and virtually no one set out on a voyage of discovery to explore the world beyond Europe's borders. The result was a lack of curiosity about the universe and an almost fatalistic acceptance of the world as it appeared—traits absent from the world of ancient Greece or Rome. As much as anything else, the contrast between the glories of the classical era and the sluggishness of medieval Europe was what created the Renaissance.

Chapter 2

Trade and the Renaissance

The Renaissance was primarily an intellectual and cultural movement centered on ideas, art, and philosophy. But there was more to the Renaissance than that. Indeed, the era got its start in large part because of practical considerations—in particular, through improvements in commerce. The people of the Renaissance revitalized Greek and Roman trade routes that had fallen into disuse. They sent cargo ships and trading caravans throughout Europe and beyond in search of necessities and luxuries alike. Moreover, the emphasis on trade led to a new sophistication in banking, bookkeeping, and other areas of finance. To understand the Renaissance, it is necessary to understand the growth of commerce that helped get the period under way.

Italy and the Mediterranean

Like most other aspects of the Renaissance, the development of commerce during this time got its start in what is now Italy. That was no accident. The Italian Peninsula sticks out several hundred miles into the heart of the Mediterranean Sea, the body of water that marks the southern boundary of Europe. Surrounded on three sides by water, the people of the peninsula looked to the sea to make their living; thus, sending cargo ships to other harbors around the Mediterranean was a natural course of action. Italy's specific location within the Mediterranean region, moreover, gave it a particular advantage where trade was concerned. For one, it extends much of the way from Europe to the African coastline. For another, Italy is about halfway between the eastern and western ends of the Mediterranean. As a result, nearly everywhere in the Mediterranean is a relatively short trip from much of Italy.

There was plenty of maritime history in the cities of Italy, too. When the Roman Empire was flourishing, ships from the larger towns of the Italian Peninsula had been especially active on the Mediterranean. Roman ships had sailed regularly from Italian ports to places such as Greece, Spain, Egypt, and Morocco. Some were commercial vessels, which carried goods for trade and sale. Others were warships, which carried soldiers. So common were Roman fighting ships and trading boats in the Mediterranean at the peak of Roman power that the sea was often known as a "Roman lake"[16]—a reference to the Roman Empire's domination of the Mediterranean.

But when the western Roman Empire began to fall apart in the 300s and 400s, so too did Roman control of the Mediterranean. As Constantinople grew larger and more powerful, its ships began taking over some of the trade that had once been Rome's, especially in the eastern part of the sea. And during most of the Middle Ages the western Church actively discouraged Christians from engaging in commerce. Though official Church disapproval did not stop every would-be merchant, the Church's general hostility toward trade certainly did not steer people into that field during medieval times.

Perhaps most important, though, the collapse of Rome dramatically reduced the demand for goods in western Europe. The peoples who defeated Rome had little use for—or interest in—the great achievements of Roman culture: the roads, the architecture, the complex economy. The interconnected society of the Roman Empire, where trade was essential and where consumer goods were much in demand, soon gave way to a society much more heavily based on subsistence agriculture, in which goods were less available and in which few people had the wherewithal to buy things. "The 'barbarian' states that occupied Italy, France and Spain," writes historian Angus Konstam, "did little to develop their economies, and consequently there was no return to the commercial heyday"[17] of the Roman Empire.

Still, the cities of the Italian Peninsula never gave up a maritime way of life. Even during the heart of the medieval era, cities such as Naples and Genoa continued to send ships out into the Mediterranean. Cargo vessels, in particular, traveled to places like Greece and North Africa, and Italian trading ships even traveled around the coast of Spain and into the Atlantic Ocean. And at various times during the 1100s and 1200s, Italian ships were a powerful force within the Mediterranean. In 1123, for example, writes author Jack Turner, a group of Venetian warships "seized a rich Egyptian merchant fleet, plundering a fortune's worth of pepper, cinnamon, and other spices."[18] Though Italian cities by no means ruled the sea, they nonetheless made their presence known throughout the Mediterranean.

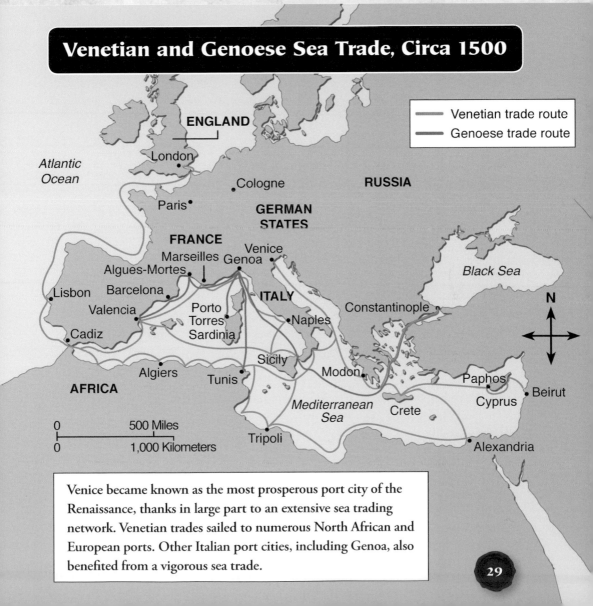

Venetian and Genoese Sea Trade, Circa 1500

- Venetian trade route
- Genoese trade route

Venice became known as the most prosperous port city of the Renaissance, thanks in large part to an extensive sea trading network. Venetian trades sailed to numerous North African and European ports. Other Italian port cities, including Genoa, also benefited from a vigorous sea trade.

"The Most Triumphant City"

Then, in the 1300s, conditions in western Europe began to change. Though the Church continued to oppose some aspects of the business world—in particular, Church leaders strongly disliked the practice of charging interest on money loaned to others—religious officials slowly relaxed their disapproval of trade as a profession. Increasingly under threat from Islamic forces to its south and east, Constantinople began to decline as a power within the Mediterranean region, allowing traders from Italy and elsewhere to gain more of a foothold. Perhaps most important, better harvests and improving economic conditions, both in Italy and elsewhere within western Europe, led to an increased demand for consumer goods. The cities of Italy had an opportunity to make significant money through trade—and they did not allow this chance to slip away.

Of all the cities that expanded their commercial activities during the early Renaissance, the most successful was unquestionably Venice. Nestled near the top of the Italian Peninsula, Venice had a number of apparent disadvantages in comparison with other cities. Most notably, Venice had very little territory. Its borders did not extend much beyond the limits of the urban area. As a result, Venice had limited agricultural capabilities, a significant problem in an era when food was scarce. But Venice had ships and a strong maritime heritage, and in the 1300s and 1400s it had ambitious and far-seeing leaders who were determined to make the best possible use of their seafaring history and their Mediterranean location.

As the people of western Europe began to clamor for trade goods, then, Venice took on the challenge of meeting that demand. Venetian merchants hurried to increase the size of their trading fleets, built new warships to protect their investments, and established what historian G.R. Potter calls "a series of strategic points, calling stations, islands and merchant quarters"[19] across much of the Mediterranean, from Spain to Lebanon and from Greece to Egypt. By bringing goods into Venice from one section of the region, then selling the goods elsewhere at higher prices, the Venetians could earn a sizeable profit. The money could then be used to upgrade ship capacities, expand

The Black Death and Economic Progress

There were several reasons for the improvements in the western European economy at the beginning of the Renaissance. One, oddly enough, was the Black Death, or bubonic plague—a deadly epidemic that affected nearly all of western Europe during the 1300s. Millions of Europeans died of the pestilence. Those who survived had to experience the deaths of their loved ones and witness the depopulation of towns and manors. The Black Death ranks among the worst disasters ever recorded in history.

But the plague also led to a higher standard of living among the survivors. During the medieval era, Europe had consistently experienced trouble feeding its people. Farms produced barely enough nourishment for everyone even in good years. As a consequence, food was scarce, and this scarcity made it expensive. Following the plague, though, the smaller population required considerably less food. With food more widely available, the cost went down. At the same time, the labor shortage that resulted from the smaller population drove wages up. Artisans and even serfs were suddenly in demand—and could therefore insist on better compensation for their work. By the end of the 1300s, Europeans were better off financially, leaving time and money for other things.

the Venetian influence further afield, or to buy luxury goods for the merchants' own use.

By the early 1400s, despite its small geographic size, Venice had become an empire of sorts: a mercantile kingdom that dominated commerce in much of the Mediterranean region. With a population approaching 100,000—an enormous number for the time—Venice was generally considered the wealthiest community west of Constantinople. Its people had a standard of living that few other Europeans of the period could begin to match. One awed observer called it "the most triumphant city I have ever seen."[20] For all Venice's success, however, it was not the only Italian city to benefit in this way from the increasing commerce. Other cities in the area, notably Genoa, Naples, and Palermo, also saw their economies flourish in the 1300s and 1400s with increased attention to trade.

Goods and Materials

The goods that moved across the Mediterranean during the early Renaissance were varied. They included raw materials such as grain, wood, and wool, and simple manufactured goods like leather, pans, and hammers. Ships laden with oats or lumber routinely entered the ports of Genoa or Venice. Most traveled short distances to and from other parts of Italy or Europe. The newly thriving trade in food, wood, and other basic supplies represented a major improvement in European life. The widespread poverty of the medieval period had stemmed in part from poor harvests and limited natural resources. But some of that poverty could have been alleviated if trade had been more common during the Middle Ages. As it was, when one part of Europe suffered from famine, there was no easy way to bring food in from other places where there was a surplus. In contrast, the burgeoning trade networks of the early Renaissance allowed merchants to deliver goods where they were needed, staving off famines and raising the standard of living throughout the continent.

In addition to the ordinary European-based trade items that traveled in and out of Italian harbors during the Renaissance, merchant ships of the time brought in a growing number of goods from outside the continent. Many of these goods could not be produced in Europe at all, and as a result they were highly prized. Much of Europe's gold, for instance, came from central Africa. Carried north to Egypt by African traders, the gold then was purchased by Italian merchants in ports such as Cairo and brought back across the Mediterranean. Other precious metals and valuable minerals also arrived in Europe from Africa, with still more originating in Saudi Arabia, Turkey, and other places.

Spices were another example. Though seasonings such as nutmeg, pepper, and cloves were in great demand throughout Europe, they grew only in tropical climates. Thus, they were imported from distant places like India and Indonesia. The spices' journey from Asia to the dinner tables of Spain or Belgium was long and involved. First they traveled overland in a trading caravan or were shipped in stages across the Indian Ocean. Eventually they made their way to Constantinople, Cairo, or another Middle Eastern port, where they were resold to traders from the Italian Peninsula. The distances were great, and the cost of the spices was correspondingly high. Indeed, the wealth of a community was sometimes measured by the amount of spices it had. "More pepper, ginger [and] nutmeg," boasted one resident of Genoa, "than in any other great city."[21]

The Spread of Commerce

Over time, the growing trade opportunities during the Renaissance changed the way Italian merchants did business. During the Middle Ages traders most often traveled from one place to another, carrying whatever goods they wished to sell. The main difference between a well-off trader and one who was barely making any money was one of scale: The poorer merchants lugged around a single cart filled with merchandise, while the richer ones had a ship at their disposal. As trade routes opened and demand for new and better merchandise grew, Italian merchants discovered they could make more money by becoming administrators, organizing trade from offices in Genoa or Venice while others did the actual work.

Accordingly, the richest merchants of the Renaissance owned not just one cargo ship but a fleet of them. They hired captains to take the ships throughout the Mediterranean and sometimes beyond. Likewise, they hired agents to represent their interests and stationed them in Egypt, Constantinople, and other commercial centers to ensure smooth transactions. There were plenty of pitfalls in practicing commerce on this scale:

A newly thriving trade in wood, basic goods, and food raised the standard of living for Europeans during the Renaissance. Expanded shipping to ports both near and far resulted in greater variety and quality of produce and spices as illustrated in this sixteenth-century painting by Joachim Beuckelaer.

A sudden storm could wipe out half a merchant's fleet, misjudging the market for a particular product could bankrupt a trader, and a bad growing season in far-off Asia could jeopardize a financier's entire wealth. Still, the potential rewards were worth the chance of disaster. As Turner notes, "If the risks were great, the profits were colossal."[22]

The increase in commerce in Italy soon spread to other parts of western Europe. One of the most important places to be affected was the Low Countries, the region made up today of Belgium and the Netherlands. Cities such as Bruges in what is now Belgium and Amsterdam in the Netherlands were centers of commercial traffic. By the late 1400s, in fact, some of these places had come to rival the trading cities of Italy. "Anyone who has money and wishes to spend it will find in this town everything that the whole world produces," Spanish traveler Pedro Tafur reported about Bruges in 1438. He noted the variety of products available in the marketplaces of the city, including Middle Eastern spices, Greek wines, and Central Asian furs. "There is no part of the world," Tafur concluded, "whose products are not found here at their best."[23]

Industry

As trade became more central in European life, manufacturing and technology rose in importance as well. Indeed, industrial growth was part of the engine that drove increasing commerce. With a rising call for goods of all kinds, but particularly finished products, entrepreneurs built mills and small factories and hurried to meet the continent's demands. Just as with commerce itself, the Italian city-states were among the first to seize the opportunity. "Venice was an important glass-making centre," writes Potter, "and also wove silk and woolen cloth."[24] The finished products were exported to other parts of Europe, further enriching the merchants of the region. Other Italian cities, notably Florence, Genoa, and Naples, developed important industries of their own.

With the passage of time, interest in manufacturing spread north and west from Italy. Towns from Portugal to Scandinavia opened factories to challenge Italy's preeminence in textile production. Spain became known for making leather, Belgium for the manufacture of beer; both products were exported across most of western Europe. The town of Solingen in what is now Germany was widely recognized for the fine swords its craftsmen produced. And the growth of technology spurred manufacturing as well. Following the invention of movable type in the mid-1400s, entrepreneurs all over northern Europe went into business making and selling paper and books. Similarly, the increasing use of gunpowder later in the Renaissance encouraged Europeans to design and build firearms, from rifles to cannons.

The rise in manufacturing led to increased commerce as goods such as swords, leather, and cloth were carried from one urban center to another. But manufacturing also led to a growing trade in the raw materials

Renaissance craftsmen of all types but especially those working with wood, cloth, leather, and metals prospered as demand for their skills and talents grew. A sixteenth-century illustration depicts one such workshop.

from which these products were made. All across Europe mines opened to dig out copper, iron, and other minerals necessary to the manufacture of armor, guns, and other metal products. In the early 1400s England sent much of its wool to Italy to be transformed into cloth. The sale of wool helped bring money into England, and eventually allowed the English to establish cloth factories of their own. Even commerce itself created a need for more raw materials. The desire for more and better ships, in particular, required the rise of new industries. As historian John Hale puts it, merchants demanded "flax for rigging and sails, iron for nails and bolts and anchors, [and] always more timber."[25]

Finance, Banks, and Wealth

The rise of commerce in the Renaissance also led to other innovations, most involving money. One of these involved keeping records of trans-actions. During medieval times, this had been a simple enough process for most traveling merchants. Since they carried most of their mer-chandise from one place to the next, they could tell at a glance what inventory they still had and what they had received for goods they had already sold. But as the complexity of trade grew, it became clear that the simple accounting methods that had worked well for a traveling merchant of the Middle Ages did not translate well to the conditions of the Renaissance. In particular, they were not sufficient to monitor the profits and losses of a wealthy Italian Renaissance trader whose three dozen ships were carrying two dozen types of goods to a dozen different ports. Something new was needed.

To meet this need, Italian merchants developed and popularized more sophisticated methods of monitoring their earnings. One of these was an accounting system known as double-entry bookkeeping. This process required merchants to record each transaction twice, providing not only a record of what funds came in and went out—and when—but also making it easy for traders to check that amounts had been recorded correctly. Though double-entry bookkeeping had been developed shortly before the Renaissance, it became extremely common during the 1400s and early 1500s. "Besides helping to make businesses more profitable," writes historian Sandra Sider, "double-entry bookkeeping, with its supporting documentation, helped merchants keep better track of their inventories and other aspects of their enterprises."[26]

Money itself represented another change. Commerce in the Middle Ages had relied largely on barter, or the exchange of one type of goods for another. A merchant might pay for a certain amount of wool, for example with copper or grain. The complexity of trade during the Renaissance, however, made this system less practical, and coins became more and more common. "European economies of the period were highly monetarized," notes economist R.A. Houston. Because of the precious metal content of most coins, moreover, many of these coins were accepted by merchants across much of the continent, even in countries far from where they had been issued. "Swedish, Dutch, French, and English coins were in common use in seventeenth-century Scotland,"[27] writes Houston.

Along the same lines, the Renaissance saw a steady rise in banking. Despite the official disapproval of the Church, there had always been banks during the Middle Ages. Most of these banks had been small, however. With an economy based primarily on barter, there was little need for much in the way of financial services. But as cash became more and more popular, the need for a larger and more stable banking industry became obvious. Among the first Europeans to establish a modern-style bank were the Medicis, a powerful family in Florence, Italy. The Medicis lent money to entrepreneurs and political figures alike. They also established branches of their bank in other cities of western Europe, including not only other Italian cities but outlying towns such as Antwerp in Belgium as well. In a sense, then, the Medicis were among Europe's first international bankers.

The Hanseatic League

Northern Germany was a prime location for commerce. During the medieval period, various coastal city-states in the region, such as Lübeck and Bremen, had formed a loose commercial confederacy. In 1369 these cities expanded by adding several more German towns, most of them further south, and became known as the Hanseatic League.

For the next century and beyond, the Hanseatic League guided the rise of commerce in northern Europe. Representatives of these towns and cities developed trading routes in the Baltic and North Seas, cooperated with one another in exchanging goods, and used their military strength to protect trading ships from piracy. They carried goods to Russia, Scandinavia, Great Britain, and the Netherlands, where their trading network met up with the networks established by the Italians.

Most historians agree that the Hanseatic League never matched the economic success of the merchants of Italy. Nor did the traders of the Hanseatic League branch out into luxury goods quite the way Italian traders did; they tended to stick with necessities such as lumber, food, and metals. By any standard, though, the Hanseatic League was quite successful—for its members and also for ordinary citizens, who benefited from the variety of goods the traders carried.

Other banks also came into the public eye during the Renaissance. One of the best known belonged to the Fugger family of Augsburg in what is now Germany. The Fuggers got their start as weavers, merchants, and mine owners. In the mid-1400s they expanded their interests to include the lending of funds. This endeavor made them rich—and like the Medicis, politically powerful as well. "In their banking role," William Manchester writes, "they loaned millions of ducats to kings, cardinals, and . . . emperor[s], financing wars, propping up popes, and underwriting new adventures."[28] Each loan needed to be paid back with interest, and the Fuggers made an enormous fortune from these interest payments. It helped the family's political position, too, that many of Europe's most powerful leaders were more or less constantly in their debt.

By the beginning of the 1500s, the revitalization of trade routes and the increase in business activity throughout Europe had brought about major changes in western Europe. The rise in trade that began in the 1300s led directly to the establishment of banks, the construction of small factories, and a higher standard of living. At the same time, the increase in commerce that marked the Renaissance contributed to other important changes. By allowing merchants to accumulate wealth once available only to the nobility and the Church, it threatened the rigid social structure of the Middle Ages. By favoring those who ventured a long way in search of trade goods, it sparked an interest in learning about the rest of the world. And by raising the standard of living, it enabled Renaissance scholars to devote more of their energies to philosophy, education, and creativity. Without the growth in trade, the Renaissance could never have become the movement it was.

Chapter 3

Learning, Science, and Humanism

The Renaissance was fundamentally a revolution of ideas. During this period, for the first time since the classical era, European cultural leaders actively sought out new perspectives and embraced innovative ways of thinking. They challenged the mindset of the medieval world, questioning ideas which in some cases had been accepted for almost a thousand years. Intellectually curious about human behavior and the world around them, these leaders had a vision of what society could and should be like. To this end, they advocated for learning, for scientific thought, and most of all for a philosophy called humanism, which emphasized the value of individual people and applauded their accomplishments. As much as anything else, the shift toward these ideals—and particularly toward humanism—defined the Renaissance.

Petrarch and the Ancients

Culturally, the Renaissance drew its primary inspiration from the past. To the thinkers of the late 1300s and early 1400s, the greatest period in human history had been classical European civilization—the era of the ancient Greeks and Romans. These thinkers admired classical philosophy, classical oratory, classical education, and much more. They looked to the Greeks and Romans for direction and viewed antiquity as a guide for addressing life's problems and concerns. Around 1450, for example, an Italian scholar and traveler named Cyriac of Ancona wrote that his generation's great responsibility was "to revive the glorious things that were alive to those living in antiquity but had become buried and defunct . . . to bring them from the dark tomb to light, to live once more."[29]

Cyriac of Ancona was not unusual in his reverence for the classical era. Nor was he by any means the first thinker of the Renaissance to express such sentiments. Most historians agree that this honor goes instead to an Italian writer named Francesco Petrarca, usually known as Petrarch in English. Born in Italy in 1304, Petrarch had a strong interest in the Greeks and Romans even in childhood. As a young man, he sought out manuscripts by classical writers in archives and monasteries across Europe. Petrarch then used his status as a well-respected man of letters to distribute copies of these works through-out Europe. Most of the Roman works had been written in Latin, which presented no barrier to Petrarch; nearly all educated western Europeans during the Middle Ages knew Latin. Greek was another story. But though Petrarch did not read Greek, he encouraged friends and acquaintances who did to translate the works of Greek writers such as Homer, Plato, and Aristotle.

Petrarch was drawn to virtually all the writers and thinkers of antiquity. He singled out Plato for particular praise, calling him "the prince of philosophers."[30] Indeed, one of Petrarch's proudest possessions was an original edition of Plato's work. Petrarch also appreciated the works of classical figures such as the Greek mathematician and philosopher Pythagoras, best known today for the geometric theorem that bears his name, and the Roman poet Virgil, best known today for his epic poem the *Aeneid.* Of all classical thinkers, though, Petrarch was most drawn toward a Roman orator, lawyer, and philosopher named Marcus Tullius Cicero. "I admire him so much," Petrarch wrote once, "that I wonder [about] people who do not admire him."[31]

Improving Society

The works of writers like Virgil, Cicero, and Plato, as Petrarch saw it, were not merely good literature; they represented a key to building a better and more vibrant culture. In Petrarch's opinion, the classical era was far superior to his own. He appreciated the ideals and the morals

The Protestant Reformation

The Protestant Reformation was a religious movement in which many European Christians broke away from papal authority. The Reformation began in 1517, when a German monk named Martin Luther challenged Church teachings and charged that the Roman hierarchy was corrupt. In the end, he and many followers founded Protestantism, a group of faiths that today encompasses Methodists, Baptists, Lutherans, and many other Christian denominations.

The Reformation took place toward the end of the Renaissance. However, historians often separate the two events; that is, they do not analyze the Reformation as a central achievement of the Renaissance but as an important movement on its own terms. Certainly there are important differences between the two. Luther and his allies focused on religion, for example, while the humanists of the Renaissance were attempting to create a more secular world. Likewise, the thinkers of the Reformation drew little inspiration from the classical era.

However, the Reformation and the Renaissance did have some ideas in common. Like the humanists, Lutheranism emphasized the role of the individual. Luther suggested, moreover, that people should read the Bible for themselves, a recommendation that dovetailed nicely with the Renaissance's emphasis on individualism, education, and literacy. And though Protestantism was a Christian movement, many humanists applauded Luther for creating a less hierarchical and less corrupt church. In these ways, the Reformation, different though it was, was a part of the Renaissance.

of antiquity as expressed by these and other writers and saw in them a blueprint for the way society should be. In particular, he admired how classical writers celebrated human achievement, human possibility, and the human powers of speech, reason, and creativity. As Petrarch saw it, society needed to emulate the ancient Greeks by emphasizing the power and creativity of humanity.

The ancient view, however, was not in tune with the medieval world. Petrarch's own time did not much value human achievement for its own sake. The standard medieval conception of the world held that people existed largely to glorify God, and that life on earth was simply preparation for the afterlife. The great works of art and literature produced during the Middle Ages had been created to praise God, not to show off the skills of their makers, and most forms of innovation had been discouraged. To Petrarch, though, the medieval way of looking at the world was flawed, and it caused him much distress. "I would rather have been born in another time,"[32] he once wrote.

Many of Petrarch's writings, then, express a desire to transform medieval society into a modern version of ancient Greece and Rome. Thus, Petrarch frequently wrote about the need for the Italians of his day to recognize and applaud human achievement and ingenuity. He also stressed the value of the individual, advocated for education, and suggested that people think for themselves about humanity's role in the universe. "What is the use, I beseech you," he demanded in one essay, "of knowing the nature of quadrupeds, fowls, fishes, and serpents, and not knowing or even neglecting man's nature [and] the purpose for which we were born?"[33] Petrarch believed wholeheartedly that striving toward these goals would bring back the splendors of the classical world and lead to an Italy that was stronger, better, and more responsive to its citizens.

Humanism

Many of Petrarch's ideas soon began to take hold in Italy. In part this was due to his voluminous correspondence; he wrote letters to dozens of important people in Italy and elsewhere during his lifetime, most of

Francesco Petrarca—poet, writer, philosopher, and scholar—dedicated his life to the pursuit of knowledge, especially from the classical world of ancient Greece and Rome. He particularly admired how the classical writers celebrated human achievement and human possibility.

them filled with new ideas. Finding Petrarch's arguments well-reasoned and admiring his passion and enthusiasm, more and more people began seeking out classical literature for themselves. At the same time, they started to adopt some of Petrarch's more compelling ideas about human achievement, the value of the individual, and the ability of humanity to shape its own destiny. Over time a new philosophy emerged. Called *humanism* today, it is based largely on principles sketched out by Petrarch, and it became the central worldview on which the Renaissance was founded.

Humanism suggests a worldview in which humans are placed at the center—a perspective in which every activity, from commerce to the arts, is viewed as part of the breadth of human experience. During the Renaissance, the humanist view placed great importance on the gathering of knowledge, but an even greater emphasis on the questioning of conventional wisdom and the ability to reason independently. Likewise, Renaissance humanists believed in the power and strength of humans to move beyond the limitations of an ordinary life. According to the humanist perspective, people are not two-dimensional characters, subject to God's whims, but thinking, feeling creatures, capable of making decisions based on observation and evidence, and born with a desire—and an ability—to create.

In addition to the emphasis on these characteristics, humanism encompassed a variety of other traits. For one, humanists believed in service to the community. Many humanists, especially early in the Renaissance, sought out roles in government and other aspects of civic life. Similarly, humanism was closely associated with the rise of republicanism, or the notion that the role of kings should be diminished in favor of rulers more answerable to the people. Both republicanism and the notion of civil service were popular in the Roman Empire, and particularly in ancient Greece; thus it made sense that humanists were drawn to these activities.

Like the Greeks and Romans before them, humanists also valued eloquence and oratory. Most humanist thinkers of the Renaissance believed that speeches were an especially effective way of convincing people to follow a particular course of action. Not just any speech would do, though. As the humanists saw it, a compelling argument needed to appeal not only to the minds of their listeners but to their emotions as well. In their opinion, argument based simply on dry logical analysis—the usual technique during the Middle Ages—was not likely to win converts. Accordingly, humanists studied the speeches of Cicero and other ancient orators, especially those who most obviously combined appeals to reason and emotion. The humanists then patterned their own speaking styles after these ancient thinkers.

A Secular World

Finally, the humanists' view of God represented a change from the view most common during the Middle Ages. While medieval scholars typically placed God in the center of all things, humanists did not necessarily agree. Some humanists even argued that human beings had played a much greater role than God in shaping society. As an Italian thinker named Gianozzo Manetti put it in 1452, "Everything that surrounds us is our own work, the work of man: all dwellings, all castles, all cities, all the edifices throughout the whole world, which are so numerous and of such quality that they resemble the works of angels."[34] The notion that humans could shape their own fate and think for themselves was sometimes called secularism; the word *secular* implies *of the world* rather than *of God*. The humanists' secularism was an important part of their overall way of thinking.

The secularism that marked the Renaissance did not mean that the humanists rejected Christianity. On the contrary, most humanists considered themselves to be strong Christians. Petrarch's enthusiasm for Christianity, for example, superseded his passion for Greece and Rome. "When we come to think or speak of religion," he wrote, "that is, of supreme truth and true happiness, and of eternal salvation, then I am certainly not a Ciceronian, or a Platonist, but a Christian." He believed, moreover, that even the ancients might have found truth and wisdom in Christianity. "Cicero himself would have been a Christian," he argued, "if he had been able to see Christ and to comprehend His doctrine."[35]

The humanists saw no contradiction between their views of the world around them and Christian thought. They firmly believed, as Christianity taught, that God had made the world. Therefore, they agreed with the Church that all creativity fundamentally came from God. Where medieval scholars had seen human creativity mainly as a

Petrarch and Introspection

Compared with writers of the late medieval era, the writers of the Renaissance were unusually introspective. They examined their thoughts and feelings in a noticeably modern way. The following excerpt, from Petrarch's autobiographical "Letter to Posterity," demonstrates some of this self-reflective quality.

I have always possessed an extreme contempt for wealth; not that riches are not desirable in themselves, but because I hate the anxiety and care which are invariably associated with them. I certainly do not long to be able to give gorgeous banquets. . . . On the other hand, the pleasure of dining with one's friends is so great that nothing has ever given me more delight than their unexpected arrival, nor have I ever willingly sat down to table without a companion. . . .

I possessed a well-balanced rather than a keen intellect, one prone to all kinds of good and wholesome study, but especially inclined to moral philosophy and the art of poetry. . . . My style, as many claimed, was clear and forcible; but to me it seemed weak and obscure. In ordinary conversation with friends, or with those about me, I never gave any thought to my language. . . . When, however, the subject itself, or the place or listener, seemed to demand it, I gave some attention to style, with what success I cannot pretend to say; let them judge in whose presence I spoke. If only I have lived well, it matters little to me how I talked.

Quoted in Jon E. Lewis, ed., *A Documentary History of Human Rights*. New York: Carroll and Graf, 2003, pp. 176–77.

very weak version of God's own powers of creation, however, the humanists argued that human creativity was much closer to God's. It was not so much Christianity that the humanists objected to but the medieval expression of it. As scholar Isabel Rivers puts it, the humanists' true goal was not to put God aside but rather "to harmonise classical ethics with the practical Christianity of the gospels."[36] The result was a blend of styles and ideas that were not nearly as opposed to each other as they sometimes appeared.

The Humanist Doctrine Spreads

Petrarch may have been the first true humanist, but he was not the last. The new doctrine spread first across the rest of the Italian Peninsula. Italy's well-known humanist writers included Colucci Salutati, another collector of early manuscripts who also served in the government of Florence; Leonardo Bruni, considered one of the first modern historians; and Niccolò Machiavelli, a diplomat and author credited with being the first truly modern political philosopher. By the later 1400s, though, the center of humanist thought had moved north, and the leading humanist writers included Johann Reuchlin, a German scholar who helped revitalize the study of Greek and Hebrew in Europe, and Thomas More, a nobleman noted for his connections—and conflicts— with King Henry VIII of England.

Probably the most important humanist writer of the later Renaissance was a Dutch philosopher known as Desiderius Erasmus. Born in the Netherlands in 1466, Erasmus was ordained a priest as a young man and remained loyal to the Church throughout his life. His great interest, however, was scholarship. Through a combination of seriousness and satire, he emphasized humanist virtues and ideals in his writings and preached the values of classical literature, tolerance, and keeping an open mind. Most of all, perhaps, Erasmus was a teacher who expanded the reach of humanism to people who were not themselves scholars. "With his irresistible need of teaching and his sincere love for humanity and its general culture," writes historian Johan Huizinga, "Erasmus introduced the classic spirit . . . among the people."[37]

Nor were all the humanists primarily writers. Some of the most famous humanists of the time were tinkerers, innovators, and scientists. Humanism was not specifically concerned with scientific progress. But the value that humanists placed on human achievement and the deep interest they had in knowledge and the world around them helped spur thinkers of the Renaissance toward inquiry and invention. Though modern scholars do not agree on how much scientific innovation the Renaissance actually produced, the period was notable for several important technological discoveries and for a newly developing emphasis on scientific thought.

Science and Technology

The best-known of these tinkerers and scientists today is Leonardo da Vinci. Born in Italy in 1452, Leonardo is remembered in large part for his art, but he also carried out dozens of experiments related to science and technology. Leonardo made an exhaustive study of human anatomy, for example, and compared the skeletal and muscular structures of human beings with those of other animals; in the process he made some important discoveries about the human body. Leonardo was also a talented engineer. He planned a series of movable walls to help protect Venice from invasion, for example, and he designed bridges, weapons, and other devices as well.

Nicolaus Copernicus, a Polish astronomer, was another scientist of the Renaissance era. Born in 1473, Copernicus grew up well versed in the astronomical principles of his time. Like other scholars of his period he believed that the sun, stars, and planets all revolved around the earth. This assumption, though wrong, had been accepted by scientists of the classical era as well. In 1514, after years of painstaking observation, complex calculations, and careful thought, Copernicus began to realize that the earth actually revolved around the sun. Worried that he would attract scorn or worse from scholars and religious authorities, however, he delayed publishing his ideas until much later. Nonetheless, Copernicus's discovery ranks among the most important in the history of science.

Innovators of the Renaissance, likewise, developed new and improved technologies in dozens of other areas. These included making gunpowder, building ships, and creating maps. But the most important innovation of the time was the invention of movable type—an achievement that made the printing press a reality. Movable type was the creation of a German goldsmith and entrepreneur named Johannes Gutenberg. Gutenberg's first working press was developed about 1440; by 1500 the technology had spread across western Europe and beyond. Over the next 60 years, European presses printed 20 million books. Printing technology allowed literate people all across Europe to own books at relatively little expense. As a result, ideas spread much more quickly than ever before. As historian Andrew Skinner writes, "The European invention of movable-type printing was, perhaps, the single most important development in the history of Western civilization . . . up to the nineteenth century."[38]

Humanism and Education

Humanism also played an important role in education. During the early medieval period education had been accessible to only a few. The sons of nobles often received basic instruction from private tutors in reading, writing, and math, and many Church leaders received a broader education with an emphasis on Church history, logic, and theology. In the latter half of the medieval era, however, education became more generally available with the rise of universities. The University of Bologna in Italy, for example, opened in 1088, and the University of Paris got its start in the early 1200s. By the late Middle Ages at least a dozen universities, most of them in France and Italy, were enrolling students.

During the Renaissance, new universities continued to open across western Europe. In 1409 the University of Leipzig opened in Germany; in 1451 the University of Glasgow was founded in Scotland. At the end of the 1400s universities were operating even in small and remote countries such as Slovakia, Belgium, and Denmark. These universities all shared several important features. They had some autonomy—that is, they were not required to do exactly what civil or Church authorities told them to

The invention of movable type made possible one of the most important innovations of the Renaissance: the printing press. Its inventor, Johannes Gutenberg, checks a proof sheet in his workshop in this undated color engraving.

do. They drew students from all over Europe, not just from their own community. And they hired their instructors from a group of scholars and teachers who were recognized authorities in their fields. These features still exist in the university systems of Europe and North America.

The education of children became increasingly important during the Renaissance, too. As in the Middle Ages, most of this education was provided by private tutors, who offered instruction to the children of wealthy nobles and merchants. However, the number of children engaged in formal learning rose during the Renaissance, partly because more people could afford to hire tutors for their children but also for practical reasons. Society during the Renaissance was growing more and more complex. The ability to read, write, and do mathematics was increasingly vital for success in a world where commerce ruled and government bureaucracy was beginning to develop.

But the rise in education for children was also due in part to the rise in humanist thinking. As the ideas of Petrarch, Erasmus, and other thinkers percolated through Europe, more and more people assimilated the humanist message that education was important for its own sake—that good citizens learned as much as they could about the world around them. Humanists even developed a model curriculum of sorts, though it is not clear how many teachers followed it. This course of study included classes in grammar, ethics, oratory, poetry, history, and Latin. "While the body was to be kept fit by exercise," summarizes John Hale, "lessons were to shape the pupil's character and prepare him for a life of useful service."[39] The specific course of study, though, was less important than the greater goal: a new emphasis on education, critical thinking, and the gathering of knowledge.

Laying a Foundation

From Petrarch to Erasmus, the great humanist thinkers of the Renaissance laid a theoretical foundation for the era. Without neglecting the creativity of God, they stressed that humans were also creative and capable of great achievements. While not denying the existence of an afterlife, they encouraged people to celebrate the delights of the current world. They championed a spirit of inquiry and a broader, more practical educational system; they drew from what they saw as the best of the past and blended it with new ideas about the future. Humanism was fundamentally responsible, then, for bringing about most of the intellectual, cultural, and spiritual changes associated with the Renaissance.

Chapter 4

Art and the Renaissance

If the people of the Renaissance had accomplished nothing else, the period would still be famous—and justly so—for its art. Throughout the Renaissance the visual arts, especially painting, sculpture, and architecture, flourished in a way never before seen in Europe. In comparison with the art of the Middle Ages, in particular, the art of the Renaissance represented a major step forward. Where the paintings of the medieval period had often appeared flat and static, for example, the painters of the Renaissance used color, perspective, and background to produce lifelike and eye-catching canvases. Similarly, the architects of the Renaissance experimented with form and style in ways rarely seen during the Middle Ages, and the sculptures produced by Renaissance artists are likewise easy to distinguish from the works of medieval sculptors.

The artists of the Renaissance created remarkable and often memorable works. The creations of artists such as Leonardo da Vinci, Michelangelo Buonarroti, and Pieter Brueghel the Elder were often considered masterpieces in their own time, and most are still viewed that way today. Centuries after their creation, Renaissance artworks such as Leonardo's *Mona Lisa* and Michelangelo's *David* represent a pinnacle of artistic achievement. For many modern critics the Renaissance still

The Renaissance is often described as an era of unparalleled artistic achievement. One of the most heralded artworks of the period is Leonardo da Vinci's Mona Lisa.

stands as a period of unparalleled creativity in art. As art historian Irene Earls writes, for example, Renaissance painters "carried painting to a peak of perfection."[40] But the importance of Renaissance art goes well beyond the artistic merit of the works these artists produced. The art of the Renaissance, at its most basic, represented a new way of looking at the world. The sculptures and paintings of the period reflected the shift from the poor, pessimistic, and superstitious Middle Ages to a period marked by hope, curiosity, and an embrace of all things human. From Italy and Spain to Germany and England, the artists of the Renaissance tackled new subjects, new techniques, and new ideas—and developed a new purpose for their artwork as well. In this way, the artists of the Renaissance not only changed artistic traditions but changed how people thought about the universe and their role in it. As Earls puts it, "The Renaissance artists gave us the first believable pictures of the world in which we live."[41]

Art and Commerce

In one sense, the brilliance of Renaissance art was made possible by much more mundane changes in the European world of the time. In particular, there was a direct link between the rise of commerce in 1300s Italy and the burst of artistic activity around the same time. As trade increased, merchants, bankers, and rulers grew ever richer. Many of the newly wealthy liked to spend their earnings in ways that showed off their affluence. Most often that meant buying luxury goods. By the late 1300s merchants and other well-off citizens of Italian cities were spending lavishly on food, clothing, furniture, and other items. The wealthy of the era, noted a writer from the Italian city of Siena, "should always seek to outdo what has been done by others on similar occasions. His country houses must be magnificent and splendid, the gardens sumptuous, the town house grand and splendid and furnished in accordance with his degree [social status] and something over."[42]

The wealthy of the early Renaissance had good reasons to spend so heavily on luxury. The increasing amount of money flowing into Europe was breaking down the old social order. During the Middle

Art and Future Generations

In addition to art being a good way for patrons to flaunt their riches, many Renaissance-era patrons saw sponsorship of art as a way to leave a personal legacy. Despite their high status and extensive wealth, these merchants and nobles recognized that fame did not endure forever. Within a few generations, they knew, they might easily be forgotten. To forestall this fate they were eager to associate themselves with something more lasting than a warehouse full of trade goods or a strongbox filled with coins. Often, that took the form of art. An important painting, an innovative palace, a beautifully carved sculpture—these objects would survive and might be admired through many generations. By commissioning and even helping to design a great work of art, a well-off merchant or nobleman might have his name—and good works—remembered forever.

Religious leaders, too, supported artists in part because they believed such patronage would reflect well on the Church. "Immortal artistic achievements," points out historian William Manchester, "would dignify the papacy and tighten its grip on Christendom." Through its support of artists like Michelangelo and Raphael, then, the Church could make it clear that it was a discerning institution with excellent artistic taste and enough money to afford any artist's fee. Equally important, though, by sponsoring works such as Leonardo's *Last Supper*, Church officials could be assured that their own largesse would be remembered favorably, too.

William Manchester, *A World Lit Only by Fire*. Boston: Little, Brown, 1992, p. 87.

Ages, social status had been a function of birth. With few exceptions, social prestige derived from being a member of the nobility. That was in part tradition, but it was also because the nobles held most of Europe's wealth. The fortunes being made by some of Italy's most successful merchants during the early Renaissance, however, changed that. As well-to-do commoners equaled—and surpassed—the wealth of noblemen, it became clear that money could buy entry into the uppermost circles of fine society. In order to take advantage of this opportunity, however, it was necessary for these newly rich financiers to make their wealth evident to everyone. Spending freely became a way of life for the upwardly mobile. As John Hale notes, "The social pressure to use surplus money to furnish and embellish was an infectious part of the age of 'more.'"[43]

Some of the well-to-do during the Renaissance contented themselves with spending their money on clothing, jewels, and country estates. But others earmarked a portion of their funds toward the purchase of artworks. Many of these buyers were in search of a sculpture, a landscape, or some other art object that would add flair to the furnishings of a home. Others were after something a bit more personal. In some places, for example, it became very nearly a requirement for wealthy merchants, nobles, and churchmen alike to pay to have their portraits painted. "It became customary in [Venice]," wrote one chronicler of the time, "that every man of any note should have his portrait painted either by Giovanni [Bellini, a well-known artist] or by some other [painter]."[44]

Over time, many of the wealthy hired the best artists again and again, commissioning these craftsmen to create pieces for the employer's own use—and sometimes supporting the artist financially while taking first pick of whatever the artist created. This system was called patronage; the person who paid for the art was known as the artist's patron. In the same way as modern corporations sponsor concert series, television programming, and baseball stadiums, the patrons of the Renaissance underwrote the costs of producing works of art, paid the creators well for their efforts—and made sure everyone knew of their largesse.

Experimentation

The concept of patronage was not entirely new to the Renaissance; most of the artists of the medieval period had worked under a patronage system, too. In the Middle Ages, though, there was in effect just one patron: the Church. In Renaissance Europe, artists who did not feel they were being treated properly by their patrons could leave that employer and sell their services elsewhere. That had not been possible during the medieval era. Not only did Church leaders control much of the wealth at the time, but the few nobles who could have afforded to hire artists typically preferred to spend their money in other ways. Artists, then, did what the Church told them to do or they found another line of work.

The medieval Church was quite specific, too, in its requests of artists. Virtually all the artworks of the Middle Ages were explicitly Christian. The bulk of medieval artworks consisted of religious materials such as paintings of saints, sculptures of Jesus, or images from the Bible. Many of these creations were designed to be a part of a church or a cathedral. Even those that were displayed in other locations, such as town squares, were most often intended to serve as a reminder of the presence of the Christian God. With few exceptions, the Church had no interest in commissioning artists to produce secular works such as portraits, paintings of everyday life, or sculptures of figures from history or mythology.

This is not to say that medieval art was uninspired or ugly. On the contrary, some medieval artworks are exceptionally beautiful, and many demonstrate the same degree of creativity that marked the Renaissance. However, the domination of art by a single institution did not lend itself to innovation in either subject matter or style. Artists of the medieval period rarely created works that pushed against the boundaries of what the Church considered acceptable. Such works, they suspected, would not be lauded for their originality and creativity but would instead be dismissed for being too different from existing art. Nor did the Church place much emphasis on individuality; artists of the medieval period were seldom credited for their work. As the Church saw it, art was intended for the glory of God, not the glory of the individual artist.

Renaissance artists explored humanist themes while still creating work that reflected their Christian faith. In La Pietà, *a work of extraordinary beauty, the sculptor Michelangelo portrays the Virgin Mary holding the lifeless body of Jesus but also shows a mother's deep sorrow at the loss of her child.*

Even in the early part of the Renaissance, much of this attitude persisted. Many of the period's great artworks remained distinctively Christian in tone; Michelangelo's sculpture *La Pietà* and Leonardo's painting *The Last Supper* are two well-known examples. But there were important changes. With a multiplicity of patrons eager for art, there was an increasing diversity of opinion about appropriate styles and subjects, even for specifically Christian works. An artist who wanted to experiment with a new idea could now do so without worrying that the result would be rejected out of hand. And even if one patron did not think much of the work, there were others to whom it might still be sold. That led to more innovation among artists than had previously been the case.

Cooperation and Creativity

At the same time, the rising influence of nobles and merchants on the art world of the early Renaissance led to a steady increase in artworks that dealt with secular subjects. Leonardo's *Mona Lisa* is probably the most famous of these, but there are many other examples from all over Europe. The Dutch painter Hubert van Eyck, for example, produced a large number of paintings on secular themes. And architects, who had formerly devoted most of their talents to the construction of cathedrals and churches, now found themselves spending more and more time planning palaces, bank buildings, and government halls. This change, too, led to greater creativity among artists and a broader understanding of what constituted acceptable art.

With the passage of the years, moreover, the relationship between artist and patron underwent some changes. Early in the Renaissance, patrons often followed the lead of the medieval Church by telling the artist exactly what they wanted, right down to size, color, and subject matter. Soon, though, patrons recognized that artists often worked best when they were involved in the planning as well as the execution of the art they created. The process, then, became increasingly collaborative. "A patron might have wanted a palace to signal his (less frequently her) status, or an image to highlight a battle victory," write authors Jonathan Katz Nelson and Richard Zeckhauser, describing how artists and patrons worked together. In turn, they add, "the architect, sculptor, or painter . . . might have proposed solutions that the [patron] literally could not have imagined."[45] The result was a cooperative energy that was much less common in the more tightly controlled world of the Middle Ages.

These changes in the way artists were viewed eventually affected even Church officials. By the early 1500s popes and bishops were beginning to modify their thinking about art and artists. Indeed, some of the masterpieces of the Renaissance were commissioned by Church leaders—and many of these patrons were content to leave at least some of the planning to the artists. During the early 1500s, for example, Pope Julius II hired Michelangelo to paint scenes from the Bible on the ceiling of the Sistine Chapel in the Vatican. Though the two men often disagreed with one another, sometimes violently—according to one story, the pope once threatened to throw Michelangelo off a platform if he did not work faster—the evidence suggests that the creation of the paintings was collaborative. "It is probable that the complex structure of the ceiling represents the prophetic visions that Julius was able to express to Michelangelo," writes historian Bard Thompson. "Michelangelo, in turn, was able to realize [Julius's ideas] on the ceiling by his artistic imagination."[46]

Some works of art commissioned by Renaissance-era Church leaders were not especially Christian in their subject matter. In addition to hiring Michelangelo to paint biblical scenes on the chapel ceiling, for example, Julius II hired another Italian artist, Raphael, to paint several frescoes on the walls of the pope's suites. The most famous of these paintings, known as *The School of Athens*, highlights ancient Greeks such as Aristotle, Euclid, and Plato as well as making reference to Renaissance artists such as Leonardo. Figures from the Bible, in contrast, are notably absent from the fresco, as are popes, theologians, and saints. Nonetheless, Julius was pleased with the work.

The Artists

The new way of thinking about art and artists extended not only to the patrons, both religious and secular, but to the artists themselves. The painters, sculptors, and architects of the Renaissance were increasingly different from the artists of the medieval era. Rather than wait for potential patrons to come to them, they promoted themselves in ways that would have been rare in the Middle Ages. Through word of mouth, many of the great artists of the time made it known that

Artists Behaving Badly

Many of the great artists of the Renaissance were arrogant, erratic, and difficult. Michelangelo's quarrels with Julius were famous, and though Julius could be inflexible, Michelangelo was equally stubborn, argumentative, and self-centered. Quite a few artists had brushes with scandal, too, and some were often in trouble with the law. Italian sculptor and goldsmith Benvenuto Cellini, for example, spent several stretches of his life in jail for crimes ranging from embezzlement to murder. These behaviors were often tolerated by the elite of the Renaissance. Despite his legal misadventures, for example, Cellini had no shortage of patrons to give him commissions. And Michelangelo, of course, continued to be admired for his creative achievements if not for his personality.

In some ways the people of the Renaissance were quite prepared to see artists behaving badly. An artist was a genius, or so the theory went, and geniuses could not be expected to adhere to ordinary standards of behavior. The passion and emotion associated with creativity, Renaissance thinkers believed, naturally led artists to throw temper tantrums over minor issues. While working on a project with Julius II, for instance, Michelangelo experienced difficulty scheduling a meeting with the pope. Furious, he left Rome. Though Michelangelo "left us without reason," as Julius explained in a letter, "we for our part are not angry with him, knowing the humours of such men of genius." To Julius, Michelangelo's outburst was a natural reaction for someone who could produce such great art.

Quoted in G.R. Potter, ed., *The New Cambridge Modern History, Volume 1: The Renaissance.* Cambridge, UK: Cambridge University Press, 1964, p. 153.

they were available for commissions. Some made direct application to patrons they particularly hoped to work for. And a few artists of the time marketed themselves in a way reminiscent of modern advertising. "Who wants some elegant little statue for their delight?" sculptors in Florence asked affluent passersby at fairs. "Our figures make every room look good."[47]

Another change involved how artists thought about their work. The artists of the Middle Ages had seen themselves as talented craftsmen. Sculptors of the medieval period, for example, were considered more or less interchangeable with bricklayers, as they both created objects from stone. During the Renaissance, however, artists began to reject that notion. Instead, they believed that their work had a different—and higher—purpose. An artist should not simply be concerned with creating practical works or works of beauty, according to this perspective, but should aim for the representation of human emotions, the sharing of human knowledge, and the speaking of truths. Artists were viewed as human and yet not quite human, because through the process of creation the artist was changed into something greater: "that divine power," as Leonardo put it, "which transforms [the artist's] mind into the likeness of the divine mind."[48]

Increasing creativity, the upsurge in self-promotion, the idea that the creation of art transformed the artist: Each of these contributed to the growing notion that an artist was a unique individual whose works were equally unique. In the medieval Church the identity of the artist had mattered very little. No one much cared who designed a particular baptismal font, created a specific stained glass window, or painted a given scene from the Bible on a church wall. In the Renaissance, however, the identity of the artist did matter. Indeed, it mattered very much. In use of color, in composition, in subject matter, the works of any two painters of the time differed widely. Similarly, sculptors and architects began more and more to put their own distinctive stamps on their work. Patrons of the Renaissance vied with each other to find artists whose work especially pleased them.

And as patrons developed their artistic tastes, their estimation of individual artists rose accordingly. Patrons often went out of their way to keep their prized artists happy. King Henry VIII of England, for example, served as patron to German painter Hans Holbein, whose abilities he much admired. When a nobleman in Henry's court lodged a complaint against Holbein, Henry made it clear that he valued Holbein far more than the nobleman, the lord's higher social status notwithstanding. "I tell you, of seven peasants I can make as many lords," he informed the complainant, "but not one Holbein." In addition, Henry warned the lord not to carry the quarrel any further. "I shall look on any injury offered to the painter as done to myself,"[49] he added.

The identity of the artist was important to the patrons of the Renaissance for esthetic reasons. While Henry admired Holbein's overall artistic ability, he was also drawn to the painter's particular style,

The biblical scenes painted on the Sistine Chapel ceiling (pictured) may represent a collaborative effort between the man who commissioned the work, Pope Julius II, and the painter, Michelangelo. Collaboration between artist and patron represented a new way of thinking about art.

which included a sense of realism and a strong emphasis on lines. But the artist's identity also had importance for social reasons. A wealthy banker of Florence or nobleman of Amsterdam preferred to be associated with a Michelangelo, Holbein, or other acknowledged genius than with an obscure journeyman whose works were indistinguishable from those of countless others. The benefits of sponsoring a particular artist, then, varied with the artist's reputation and fame.

Humanism and Art

The art of the Renaissance was undeniably beautiful. Technically speaking, it was highly sophisticated as well. Renaissance structures such as St. Peter's Basilica in Rome and the City Hall of Antwerp, Belgium, are justly known for their gracefulness, their balance, and their precision. Renaissance sculptures from Benvenuto Cellini's gold miniatures to Michelangelo's larger-than-life marble statues are likewise famous for their attention to detail and their focus on form. And Renaissance paintings by masters such as Raphael, Albrecht Dürer, and Van Eyck not only strike the eye with their use of color and their treatment of light, but show an advanced understanding of perspective, composition, and other painting techniques.

But the art of the Renaissance was about much more than simple beauty or innovative techniques. Its main impact lies, instead, in its meaning for the culture that produced it. The Renaissance was a time of intellectual and philosophical change, a period in which people focused on new ways of thinking about themselves and the world around them—and the art of the era reflected these new realities. Renaissance artworks based on biblical and other religious themes were intended in part for the glory of God, just as they had been during the Middle Ages. But more and more, the art of the Renaissance was meant to highlight the glories of humanity. In addition to pleasing the eye, then, the art of the period emphasized the possibilities in human endeavor, the range of human experience, and the worth of the individual.

The emphasis on these human qualities is easy to find in the art of the Renaissance. Works such as Raphael's *School of Athens* encouraged people to look not simply to God for inspiration but to the great ideas of past and present civilizations as well. Portraiture became a popular art form during the period. Modern scholars agree that Renaissance artists were drawn toward portraiture, as Thompson puts it, as "a means of expressing the uniqueness, importance, and psychological complexity of a human being."[50] Similarly, Michelangelo's *The Creation of Adam*, on the Sistine Chapel ceiling, places Adam as very nearly on the same level as God. Paintings and sculptures took on a new realism, approximating more and more the experiences of real life. In this way, the art of the Renaissance was in some sense the most humanistic of all the features that marked the era.

Chapter 5

What Is the Legacy of the Renaissance?

The Renaissance was certainly an important period in its own right. The changes in society, art, and philosophy that took place during the late 1300s and beyond were enormous and often dramatic. The rise in wealth, the increase in technological sophistication, the spread of humanist ideals, the brilliant artworks of the period—all help make the Renaissance one of the most vital eras in European history. The Renaissance was perhaps especially remarkable for the sheer amount of change it brought and the rapidity with which those changes took place. As historian Anne Denieul-Cormier writes, the Renaissance was "the crucible in which a new civilization was being synthesized."[51]

The changes the Renaissance ushered in, moreover, affected the lives of millions of people across Europe at the time. Some were merchants who enjoyed a higher standard of living; others were artists eager to develop new techniques in painting, sculpture, and building. Still others were farmers who followed the economic shifts of the time by leaving the countryside and looking for jobs in cities such as Antwerp, Paris, or Milan. And certainly some people were negatively affected by the coming of the Renaissance—most notably the nobles and churchmen who began to see some of their power slip away in favor of the newly wealthy merchants, bankers, and entrepreneurs. Whether they came out ahead or behind, however, much of the European population at the time experienced major shifts in their lives as new ideas and perspectives took hold and old ones faded away.

But the influence of the Renaissance goes a great deal further than the mid-1500s, when most historians agree it reached its end. In fact, the Renaissance has affected far more lives since it ended than it affected when it was in full flower. From science to politics and from art to philosophy, the Renaissance had an impact on virtually all aspects of human existence during its own time and has continued to influence life in dozens of ways even into the present day. Few civilizations have retained such an imposing presence so many years later. The civilizations of Europe in the Renaissance is one of those few.

Business and Trade

One of the most important effects of the Renaissance had to do with commerce. Throughout the Renaissance the volume of trade in and out of Europe climbed steadily. When the era was over, however, European commerce did not drop. On the contrary, it continued to rise. One reason was that trade had helped the people of the Renaissance build enormous fortunes. During the Renaissance struggling merchants had become affluent, and well-off capitalists had become wealthy beyond all imagination. The rich of the post-Renaissance world wanted to continue trading in order to increase their fortunes even further. At the same time, the less affluent saw the commercial world as their quickest route to wealth. The result was a flood of Europeans eager to make their mark in the business world. They had learned the lessons of the Renaissance well.

Another reason for the continued commerce involved consumers. The Europeans of the Renaissance had become accustomed to owning goods from across Europe and beyond—goods unavailable, or nearly so, just a century or two earlier. By the 1600s middle-class Europeans as well as nobles were unwilling to live without imported goods such as spices, cloth, and copper. "The demand increased for silverware and ceramics and glass," writes John Hale about the post-Renaissance period, "for Persian and Turkish rugs to give a colourful glow to tables;

for Flemish and French, and then Florentine and English tapestries to take the chill from the walls."[52] The typical household of the mid-1600s had many more furnishings, decorations, and clothing than its counterpart of three centuries before. The Renaissance had ushered in an age of consumerism.

The Renaissance also permanently changed the way people thought about wealth. In the medieval era, wealth for the most part meant land. People who owned a great deal of land were considered rich; those who owned no land or very little land, in contrast, were not rich and probably never would be. The merchants of the Renaissance, however, redefined the concept of wealth. Increasingly, affluence was measured not in land but in other property: luxurious goods, fine clothing, and most of all in cash. This trend continued to accelerate even after the end of the Renaissance. In addition to relying more and more on cash—including paper money—the post-Renaissance period saw the growth of a variety of new products and services related to money as well. Banks flourished, the stock market became a part of many European economies, and the economic system of capitalism got its start.

The effect of this new mercantile economy was enormous. As Europeans did more business with each other and with people in far-off countries, they grew in wealth—but they also grew in power. During the Middle Ages western Europe had been an afterthought. Scientifically, culturally, and militarily, it could not compete with Constantinople or other great cities of the Middle East. But as commerce increased and prosperity became more common, western Europe became a power. Its armies were well supplied, its artistic achievements were undeniable, and its importance in global affairs was growing steadily. Once an isolated backwater, Europe by the 1600s was playing a leading role in the world—a role that only grew over the next few centuries. Without the traders of the 1300s and 1400s and the rise in standard of living that began around that time, it is hard to see how Europe could have achieved a position of such supremacy in world affairs so many years later.

Exploration and Discovery

The post-Renaissance years were also marked by a burst of exploration and discovery as Europeans traveled further and further across the earth. This period of exploration actually began during the Renaissance. A Portuguese explorer named Bartolomeu Dias, for example, made a succession of voyages that took him southward along Africa's Atlantic coast during the late 1480s. In 1498 Vasco da Gama, also of Portugal, sailed around Africa altogether and reached the western coastline of India. And Europeans headed west as well: Christopher Columbus reached the Americas in 1492, and explorers such as the Spaniards Hernán Cortés, Francisco Pizarro, and Hernando de Soto traveled into the interior of North and South America in the first years of the sixteenth century.

The pace of discovery, however, increased following the Renaissance. In the early 1600s, for example, Dutch ships began visiting the coast of Australia, while the English started to investigate what

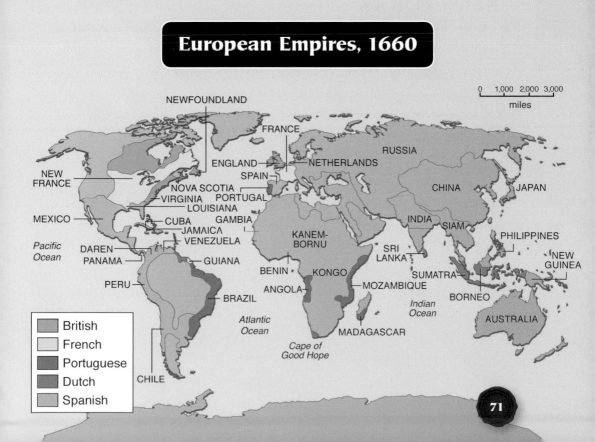

European Empires, 1660

British
French
Portuguese
Dutch
Spanish

NEWFOUNDLAND
FRANCE
RUSSIA
ENGLAND
NETHERLANDS
NEW FRANCE
SPAIN
CHINA
JAPAN
NOVA SCOTIA
VIRGINIA
PORTUGAL
LOUISIANA
MEXICO
CUBA
GAMBIA
INDIA
SIAM
JAMAICA
KANEM-BORNU
PHILIPPINES
Pacific Ocean
DAREN
VENEZUELA
SRI LANKA
NEW GUINEA
PANAMA
GUIANA
SUMATRA
BENIN
KONGO
PERU
MOZAMBIQUE
BORNEO
BRAZIL
ANGOLA
Indian Ocean
AUSTRALIA
Atlantic Ocean
MADAGASCAR
Cape of Good Hope
CHILE

0 1,000 2,000 3,000
miles

is now the Canadian Arctic. All through the 1600s and 1700s European explorers mapped and studied places as diverse as Polynesia, the North American plains, and the Indian Ocean. Constant improvements in shipbuilding, navigation techniques, and mapmaking made travel easier and easier as time went by, and the Europeans took full advantage of this opportunity. By the mid-1700s there were still parts of the world that Europeans knew very little about, but the list was dwindling rapidly.

The emphasis on exploration was related to two important traits of the Renaissance. One was the growth of commerce. Trade considerations spurred early explorers such as Dias, Columbus, and da Gama to undertake their voyages. Each hoped to find a quicker, less expensive path to the eastern parts of Asia, where valuable trade goods such as spices and silk could be had—and where canny merchants could make a fortune by going directly to the source instead of waiting for these materials to come to them. Later explorers sailed to other unknown places in a hunt for gold, silver, and other precious metals. As it happened, gold was rarely in as much supply as the explorers hoped. But trade in other items from around the globe, including cotton, potatoes, minerals, and furs, boomed following the Renaissance.

Changes in the European mindset were just as important as trade in bringing about the era of exploration. In science, art, and philosophy, the people of the Renaissance placed a high value on learning and discovery. It made sense, then, that they would have a keen interest in learning what lay outside Europe's borders. During the medieval era, mapmakers were content to fill the many blank spots on their maps with rumors and suppositions: sea monsters off the coast of Africa, a mythical Christian king (Prester John) in Central Asia, rivers and mountains that did not actually exist. The coming of the Renaissance, with its emphasis on knowledge and investigation, made mapmakers unwilling to guess any longer. Instead, they demanded facts. A society that championed intellectual curiosity was naturally supportive of those who tried to expand the knowledge of the world.

The Rise of Science

The Renaissance passion for information and discovery also had a lasting effect on science. There had been a few important scientific discoveries during the Renaissance; one of the most notable was Copernicus's realization that the earth traveled around the sun. However, the number of these discoveries rose sharply in the years following the Renaissance. The 1600s, in particular, were a time of great scientific advancement. English scientist and mathematician Isaac Newton, for example, described the basic laws of motion, developed the theory of gravity, and carried out many experiments involving light. His book *Principia Mathematica* laid out the foundations of modern science and has been called one of the most important books ever written. Newton's impact on science was so enormous, in fact, that poet Alexander Pope composed these lines about him:

> "Nature and nature's laws lay hid in night;
> God said 'Let Newton be' and all was light."[53]

Newton was particularly influential, but he was far from the only great scientist produced by Europe in the years after the Renaissance. German astronomer Johannes Kepler identified the rules that described the movements of the planets, allowing him to predict where they would be at any given time and helping him understand the various forces that caused them to move as they did. Another astronomer, Christiaan Huygens of the Netherlands, was the first to spot Saturn's most impressive feature. The planet, he wrote, "is surrounded by a thin flat ring, nowhere touching, and inclined to the ecliptic [that is, positioned diagonally]."[54] Huygens also studied the properties of light and explored the movement of pendulums. And in biology, English physician William Harvey became the first scientist to describe the human circulatory system.

Galileo Galilei of Italy was yet another astronomer and mathematician in the years following the Renaissance. He is well known today for building on Copernicus's observations to demonstrate that the earth does indeed travel around the sun. He is also famous, however, for running afoul of Church teaching with this claim. Galileo's problem was that several passages in the Bible imply that the earth is at the center of the universe. Church officials were bound to uphold this idea even in the face of Galileo's evidence to the contrary. As Manchester puts it, "Whenever observed experience conflicted with Holy Scripture, observation had to yield."[55] Church leaders eventually arrested Galileo, banned his books, and forced him to recant. The damage had been done, however. Thanks to the Renaissance invention of the printing press, copies of the books circulated throughout Europe despite the Church's best efforts to contain them.

Whether their particular interest was anatomy, physics, or mathematics, all of these scientists were directly influenced by the tinkerers and investigators of the Renaissance. The Renaissance had made it acceptable to be curious about the world and how it worked. The philosophy of the Renaissance emphasized observation and critical analysis, ideals that did not die with the end of the era but continued into the next period of history as well. Seventeenth-century scientists such as Galileo and Newton thrived in a system that valued these ideals. Though Galileo's experience indicates that not everyone in Europe accepted reason over doctrine, the amount of support he received from scientific thinkers suggests that a growing number of Europeans were doing just that. The Renaissance had changed the way Europeans thought about science, and the people of the post-Renaissance period built on these changes.

Humanism and Philosophers

Of all the changes brought about by the Renaissance, however, perhaps the most persistent involves the humanist philosophy espoused by Petrarch, Erasmus, and other thinkers. In the centuries immediately following the Renaissance, humanism became a major influence on European society—and eventually on American society as well. From

Rousseau, Locke, and Revolution

John Locke and Jean-Jacques Rousseau were both widely respected during their own times—and each had an important impact on the politics of the late 1700s as well. The French Revolution of 1789, which removed the long-standing French monarchy in favor of a democratic system of government, was based in part on Rousseau's ideas. The revolutionaries' emphasis on the rights of the lowest classes would probably have gone too far for many Renaissance humanists, who tended to champion the rights of the well-educated middle and upper middle classes rather than of the poor. Still, the revolution itself, with its focus on the natural rights of humanity, was nevertheless a logical outgrowth of the humanist ideas of thinkers like Petrarch and Erasmus.

Locke's ideas were also useful to the revolutionaries in France. However, Locke's writings made an even greater impact on revolutionaries across the Atlantic Ocean from Europe. His words inspired colonial American thinkers such as Thomas Jefferson and Thomas Paine to demand independence from England during the 1770s. Indeed, parts of the Declaration of Independence were strongly influenced by Locke. In particular, the notion that humans are by right entitled to "life, liberty, and the pursuit of happiness" was drawn almost directly from Locke's works—and would not have been alien at all to the humanists of the Renaissance.

its emphasis on observation and reason to its perspective on literature and the arts, and from its support of education to its faith in human achievement, the humanist philosophy that developed during the Renaissance stretches across the centuries. Many of the changes in the world since that time can be attributed at least partly to the impact of humanist philosophy.

The humanism of the Renaissance, for example, is easy to see in the period called the Enlightenment. The Enlightenment, often known as the Age of Reason, began in the later 1600s and continued for over a century. Like the Renaissance, the Enlightenment emphasized new ideas, the dignity and value of human beings, and the search for knowledge. Denis Diderot of France, for example, spent over 20 years compiling an encyclopedia. Diderot's project, which he completed in 1772, served as a reference work, but it had a greater purpose as well. As Diderot expressed it, he intended "to change the way people think."[56] This notion would have been familiar to many Renaissance figures, who of course wanted to reform society by replacing the medieval worldview with something very different.

The influence of the Renaissance on the Enlightenment can also be seen in the works of philosophers such as John Locke of England, born in 1632, and Jean-Jacques Rousseau, born in Switzerland in 1712. Both Locke and Rousseau, like most thinkers of the Renaissance, had a generally positive view of people and their potential. Each believed that humans were at heart tolerant, intelligent, and reasonable. Locke echoed the humanists' concerns about the power of organized religion by advocating for a separation of church and state—that is, for having a secular government in which religious leaders had no power to make laws or arrest people. Rousseau's book *Confessions*, often called the first modern autobiography, owes much to the emphasis on introspection begun by Renaissance humanists such as Petrarch.

Education, Secularism, and Technology

Modern education, too, owes much to the humanist ideas of the Renaissance. From the Renaissance into the twentieth century, schools at all levels frequently based their courses of study on classical models. For generations, for example, knowledge of Latin was expected of nearly all university graduates. Similarly, oratory (also called rhetoric) was a subject typically studied at the high school level. Today, much of the emphasis on classical studies is gone, at least in the United States, in favor of a focus on more practical subjects. Very few high school or college graduates of modern times have read Cicero

The invention of the printing press during the Renaissance had a lasting impact on people and cultures around the world. It allowed people to share ideas and information quickly and easily, which in turn contributed to rapid and enduring changes in politics, economics, and daily life.

in the original Latin, a fact that would surely disappoint Petrarch. However, it seems clear that along with other Renaissance humanists, Petrarch would applaud the easy access to schooling across the Western world today.

The secularism of the Renaissance also had an enormous legacy. Though the humanists of the Renaissance only partially succeeded in diminishing the power of organized religion, they did pioneer the idea that religion should not dominate the rest of society. Since the Renaissance, the power and influence of Christianity in the West has generally declined. Even since the days of Galileo, who ran afoul of the Church for his theory that the sun was at the center of the solar system, secularism has come a very long way. Today, to a very large extent, scientific reasoning, laws, and other aspects of Western civic and cultural life exist independently of the Bible and the doctrines of any religious body, Christian or otherwise.

Finally, the technological innovations of the Renaissance changed the world in ways both great and small. The spirit of inquiry that marked the Renaissance led not only to voyages around the world and to the setting up of new universities, but also to inventions like the printing press. By the 1600s books and other publications were everywhere. Anyone with a little money and something to say could have books or handbills printed up and distributed across a community or even beyond. By allowing people to share ideas quickly and easily, the printing press made it possible to make rapid changes in politics, economics, and more. Without the printing press, it is conceivable that the American Revolution, along with many other important events of later years, would never have taken place.

The impact of the Renaissance, then, is enormous indeed. Directly or indirectly, the new philosophies, values, and attitudes that shaped the Renaissance also shaped Europe—and indeed the whole world—in the years to come. The growth of scientific reasoning in the years since the Renaissance can be attributed in part to the values of humanism and its emphasis on knowledge. The voyages of discovery that took place in the late 1500s and beyond were a logical outgrowth of the rising importance of trade and the increasing spirit of inquiry during the Renaissance. The modern system of higher education, the sophisticated twenty-first century economic system, the elections in which voters choose the rulers of today—all of these features of modern life were set into motion by the events of the Renaissance centuries ago. The legacy of the Renaissance is everywhere.

Source Notes

Chapter One: What Conditions Led to the Renaissance?

1. Colette Hemingway and Seán Hemingway, "The Art of Classical Greece," *Heilbruun Timeline of Art History*. New York: Metropolitan Museum of Art, 2000. www.metmuseum.org.

2. UNESCO World Heritage Centre, "Acropolis, Athens." http://whc.unesco.org.

3. Quoted in David Willey, "24 August 410: The Date It All Went Wrong for Rome?," BBC News Europe, August 24, 2010, www.bbc.co.uk.

4. William McNeill, *The Rise of the West*. Chicago: University of Chicago Press, 1963, p. 538.

5. Steven Runciman, *The First Crusade and the Foundation of the Kingdom of Jerusalem*. New York: Cambridge University Press, 1980, p. 50.

6. George Holmes, *The Later Middle Ages*. Edinburgh, UK: Thomas Nelson and Sons, 1962, p. 15.

7. Quoted in Peter N. Stearns, *World History in Documents*. New York: New York University Press, 2008, p. 103.

8. Quoted in Stearns, *World History in Documents*, p. 103.

9. Jeffrey Burton Russell, *A History of Medieval Christianity*. New York: Crowell, 1968, p. 85.

10. William Manchester, *A World Lit Only by Fire*. Boston: Little, Brown, 1992, p. 22.

11. Barbara Tuchman, *A Distant Mirror: The Calamitous 14th Century*. New York: Knopf, 1978, p. 34.

12. Quoted in James A. Garrison, *Civilization and the Transformation of Power*. New York: Paraview, 2000, p. 192.

13. Manchester, *A World Lit Only by Fire*, p. 5.

14. McNeill, *The Rise of the West*, p. 539.

15. Manchester, *A World Lit Only by Fire*, p. 22.

Chapter Two: Trade and the Renaissance

16. Matthew Bunson, *A Dictionary of the Roman Empire*. New York: Oxford University Press, 1995, p. 272.

17. Angus Konstam, *Piracy: The Complete History*. Guilford, CT: Globe Pequot, 2008, p. 73.

18. Jack Turner, *Spice*. New York: Random House, 2004, p. 102.

19. G.R. Potter, ed., *The New Cambridge Modern History, Volume 1: The Renaissance*. Cambridge, UK: Cambridge University Press, 1964, p. 46.

20. Quoted in Potter, *The New Cambridge Modern History, Volume 1: The Renaissance*, p. 46.

21. Quoted in Turner, *Spice*, p. 134.

22. Turner, *Spice*, p. 105.

23. Quoted in John Hale, *The Civilization of Europe in the Renaissance*. New York: Atheneum, 1994, p. 175.

24. Potter, *The New Cambridge Modern History, Volume 1: The Renaissance*, p. 47.

25. Hale, *The Civilization of Europe in the Renaissance*, p. 172.

26. Sandra Sider, *Handbook to Life in Renaissance Europe*. New York: Oxford University Press, 2007, p. 210.

27. R.A. Houston, "Colonies, Enterprises, and Wealth: The Economies of Europe and the Wider World," in *Early Modern Europe*, ed. Euan Cameron. New York: Oxford University Press, 1999, p. 148.

28. Manchester, *A World Lit Only by Fire*, p. 50.

Chapter Three: Learning, Science, and Humanism

29. Quoted in Hale, *The Civilization of Europe in the Renaissance*, p. 191.

30. Quoted in Prudence Allen, *The Concept of Woman, Volume 2*. Grand Rapids, MI: Eerdmans, 2002, p. 261.

31. Quoted in Ronald G. Witt, *In the Footsteps of the Ancients*. Leiden, The Netherlands: Koninklijke Brill, 2000, p. 258.

32. Quoted in Hale, *The Civilization of Europe in the Renaissance*, pp. 394–95.

33. Quoted in Bard Thompson, *Humanists and Reformers*. Grand Rapids, MI: Eerdmans, 1996, p. 210.

34. Quoted in John Rigby Hale, *Renaissance*. New York: Time, 1965, p. 20.

35. Quoted in Witt, *In the Footsteps of the Ancients*, p. 258.

36. Isabel Rivers, *Classical and Christian Ideas in English Renaissance Poetry*. London: Routledge, 1979, p. 40.

37. Johan Huizinga, *Erasmus and the Age of Reformation*. New York: Dover, 2001, p. 39.

38. Andrew Skinner, *A Bible Fit for Restoration*. Springville, UT: CFI, 2011, p. 28.

39. Hale, *The Civilization of Europe in the Renaissance*, p. 194.

Chapter Four: Art and the Renaissance

40. Irene Earls, *Renaissance Art: A Topical Dictionary*. Westport, CT: Greenwood, 1987, p. xiii.

41. Earls, *Renaissance Art: A Topical Dictionary*, p. xiii.

42. Quoted in Jonathan Katz Nelson and Richard Zeckhauser, *The Patron's Payoff*. Princeton, NJ: Princeton University Press, 2008, p. 3.

43. Hale, *The Civilization of Europe in the Renaissance*, p. 267.

44. Quoted in Hale, *The Civilization of Europe in the Renaissance*, p. 265.

45. Nelson and Zeckhauser, *The Patron's Payoff*, p. 18.

46. Thompson, *Humanists and Reformers*, p. 264.

47. Quoted in Hale, *The Civilization of Europe in the Renaissance*, p. 268.

48. Quoted in Potter, *The New Cambridge Modern History, Volume 1: The Renaissance*, p. 151.

49. Quoted in *Masters in Art*, "The Drawings of Holbein the Younger." Boston: Bates and Guild, March 1902, p. 24.

50. Thompson, *Humanists and Reformers*, p. 4.

Chapter Five: What Is the Legacy of the Renaissance?

51. Anne Denieul-Cormier, *A Time of Glory: The Renaissance in France*. Garden City, NY: Doubleday, 1968, p. 12.

52. Hale, *The Civilization of Europe in the Renaissance*, p. 173.

53. Quoted in Michael Spivak, *Calculus*. New York: Cambridge University Press, 1994, p. 327.

54. Quoted in Dava Sobel, "Secrets of the Rings," *Discover*, April 1994. http://discovermagazine.com.

55. Manchester, *A World Lit Only by Fire*, p. 291.

56. Quoted in Clorinda Donato and Robert M. Maniquis, *The Encyclopedie and the Age of Revolution*. Boston: G.K. Hall, 1992, p. 11.

Important People of the Renaissance

Michelangelo Buonarroti: An Italian painter and sculptor of the Renaissance, Michelangelo created the massive sculpture *David*, which depicts a biblical king as a youth. He also painted biblical scenes on the ceiling of the Sistine Chapel in the Vatican. He is considered among the greatest artists in history.

Nicolaus Copernicus: Copernicus, a Polish-born astronomer, made the then-astonishing discovery that the sun did not actually revolve around the earth; rather, the earth moved around the sun. Because of concerns about how his work would be received, however, Copernicus chose not to publish his results until several decades after he learned the truth.

Leonardo da Vinci: A scientist, engineer, and artist, da Vinci painted the *Mona Lisa*, *The Last Supper*, and several other well-known pieces of art. He is also known for designing machines, many of which could not be built with the technology of the time, and for his studies of human anatomy.

Desiderius Erasmus: A well-known humanist of the later Renaissance, Erasmus wrote and taught widely on various topics in his native Netherlands as well as in Italy, England, and other nations. Able to use both humor and seriousness to get his points across, Erasmus is often considered the leading advocate of the humanist philosophy in the 1500s.

Johannes Gutenberg: An entrepreneur and a goldsmith from Germany, Gutenberg invented movable type—a system in which metal molds with letters and other symbols could be placed together to form words, then inked to print multiple sheets at the same time. Gutenberg's invention made the printing press feasible.

Hans Holbein: Holbein was known as one of the finest artists in Europe during the sixteenth century. Born in Germany, Holbein spent much of his professional career at the court of King Henry VIII of England. A portrait of Henry ranks among his best-known works today.

Medici family: The Medicis were a powerful Italian family with particular interests in politics and banking. They ruled the Republic of Florence for many years during the Renaissance and became wealthy by making loans to Europe's well-off citizens. Many members of the family also became patrons to Italy's most successful artists.

Francesco Petrarcha (Petrarch): An Italian poet, author, and collector of classical literature, Petrarch is often called the father of humanism or the founder of the Renaissance. His enthusiasm for the writers of antiquity helped bring them into the public eye, and his ideas on religion, rhetoric, education, and other topics were quite popular.

For Further Research

Books

Bulant Atalay, *Leonardo's Universe: The Renaissance World of Leonardo da Vinci*. Washington, DC: National Geographic, 2008.

Kenneth Bartlett, ed., *The Civilizations of the Italian Renaissance: A Sourcebook*. Toronto: University of Toronto Press, 2011.

Heather M. Campbell, ed., *The Ascent of the West: From Prehistory Through the Renaissance*. New York: Rosen, 2011.

Neil Grant, *Renaissance Europe*. Florence, Italy: McRae, 2009.

Stephen Greenblatt, *The Swerve: How the World Became Modern*. New York: W.W. Norton, 2011.

Kathryn Hinds, *Everyday Life in the Renaissance*. New York: Benchmark, 2009.

Kathleen Kuiper, ed., *The 100 Most Influential Painters and Sculptors of the Renaissance*. New York: Rosen, 2009.

Briony Ryles and Derek Hall, eds., *Medieval Period and the Renaissance*. Lakeland, FL: Brown Bear, 2010.

Websites

Da Vinci and the Renaissance (www.pbs.org/treasuresoftheworld/mona_lisa/mlevel_2/mlevel2_renaissance.html). Material about the Renaissance, provided by PBS, with a particular focus on Leonardo and his work on the *Mona Lisa*.

European Renaissance Art (www.metmuseum.org/toah/hi/hi_reneup er.htm). Extensive information about the art and artists of the Renaissance, including over 100 essays and 10 timelines. Provided by the Metropolitan Museum of Art.

Internet Medieval Sourcebook (www.fordham.edu/halsall/sbook.asp). A compilation of important texts relating to medieval and early modern Europe; also includes links to similar sites. Sponsored by Fordham University.

Printing: Renaissance and Reformation (http://library.sc.edu/spcoll /sccoll/renprint/renprint.html). Information provided by the University of South Carolina Libraries about printing and print technology during the Renaissance, with examples of text before and after Gutenberg's invention of movable type.

The Renaissance: An Overview (www.pbs.org/empires/medici/renais sance/index.html). Sponsored by PBS, a description of the Renaissance and its achievements, including links and a time line.

Selected Sources: Renaissance (www.fordham.edu/Halsall/sbook1x .asp). Texts from Renaissance writers, including Petrarch and Machiavelli, and information about Renaissance artists. Sponsored by Fordham University.

Web Gallery of Art (www.wga.hu). A virtual museum of European art, including many examples of works from the Renaissance.

Index

Note: Boldface page numbers indicate illustrations.

Acropolis (Athens), 15, **16**

Aeneid (Virgil), 42

Age of Reason (the Enlightenment), 76

Antigone (Sophocles), 15

architecture

    Greek, 15

    Renaissance, 54

    Roman, 17, 28

    Romanesque style of, 25

art/artists, 12, 54, 63

    commerce and, 56, 58

    Greek, 15

    humanism and, 66–67

    medieval versus Renaissance, 62, 64–66

    Roman, 17

    sponsorship of, 57, 58–59

banking, 38–40

Bellini, Giovanni, 58

Beuckelaer, Joachim, 34

Black Death , 25

    economic progress and, 31

bookkeeping, double-entry, 37–38

Brant, Sebastian, 12

Brueghel, Pieter (the Elder), 54

Bruni, Leonardo, 49

bubonic plague. *See* Black Death

Canterbury Tales, The (Chaucer), 12

capitalism, 70

Cellini, Benvenuto, 63

Chaucer, Geoffrey, 12

Christianity, 12, 23–25

    decline in influence of, 78

humanism/secularism and, 47, 49

influence of, on medieval worldview, 23–24

Cicero, Marcus Tullius, 17, 42, 47

Columbus, Christopher, 71

commerce, 27–28, 69–70, 72

art and, 56, 58

during the Middle Ages 33, 37, 38

Hanseatic League and, 39

innovations flowing from, 37–38

spread of, 33–35

Venice and, 30–32

See also trade/trade routes

Confessions (Rousseau), 76

Constantinople, 28, 30

consumerism, 69–70

Copernicus, Nicolaus, 13, 50, 73, 84

Cortés, Hernán, 71

Creation of Adam, The (Michelangelo), 67

Cyriac of Ancona, 41–42

da Gama, Vasco, 71

Dante Alighieri, 18

David (Michelangelo), 54

Declaration of Independence, 75

Denieul-Cormier, Anne, 68

de Soto, Hernando, 71

Dias, Bartolomeu, 71

Diderot, Denis, 76

Diocletian (Roman emperor), 17–18

discovery, voyages of, 71–72, 78–79

Dürer, Albrecht, 66

Earls, Irene, 56

education, 51–53, 76–78

Enlightenment, the (Age of Reason), 76

Erasmus, Desiderius, 49–50, 84

humanist philosophy of, 74, 75

Europe

classical era in, 10

empires of, 71

impact of Renaissance on, 70

feudal system, 20–21

  consequences of, 21–23

French Revolution (1789), 75

Fugger family, 39–40

Galileo Galilei, 73–74

Greece, ancient, 14–16

Gutenberg, Johannes, 51, 52, 84

Hale, John, 37, 53, 58, 69–70

Hanseatic League, 39

Harvey, William, 73

Hemingway, Colette, 15

Hemingway, Seán, 15

Henry VIII (king of England), 65

Holbein, Hans, 65, 85

Holmes, George, 20

Horace, 17

Houston, R.A., 38

Huizinga, Johan, 49

humanists/humanism, 11–13, 44–48

  art and, 66–67

Christianity and, 47, 49

definition of, 41, 46

education and, 51–53

Lutherism and, 43

philosophers and, 74–76

spread of, 49–50

Huygens, Christiaan, 73

industry/manufacturing, 35, 37

Italy, trade and, 27–29

Jefferson, Thomas, 75

Julius II (pope), 62, 63

Kepler, Johannes, 73

Konstam, Angus, 28

Last Supper, The (Leonardo), 57, 59, 60

Leonardo da Vinci, 13, 54, 59, 64, 84

  the Church and, 57

science and, 50

Locke, John, 75, 76

Luther, Martin, 43

Machiavelli, Niccolò, 49

Manchester, William, 22, 25, 57, 74

  on the Fugger family, 39–40

  on stagnation of the Middle Ages, 25–26

Manetti, Gianozzo, 47

maps/mapmaking, 72

  medieval, 19

McNeill, William, 18, 25

Medici family, 38, 85

Michelangelo Buonarroti, 54, 60, 67, 84

  the Church and, 57

  Julius II and, 62, 63

Middle Ages, 17–18

  art of, 54, 59

  the Church and, 23–25

  commerce during, 33, 37, 38

  feudal system of, 20–23

  maps of, 19

  stagnation of, 25–26

view of artist in, 64

Mona Lisa (Leonardo), **55**, 61

More, Thomas, 49

Newton, Isaac, 73

Ovid, 17

Paine, Thomas, 75

patrons/patronage, 57

  the Church and, 59–61

  collaboration between artists and, 64–67

Petrarch (Francesco Petrarca), 42–46, 45, 78, 85

  Christianity and, 47

  humanist philosophy of, 74, 75

La Pietà (Michelangelo), **60**

Pizarro, Francisco, 71

Plato, 42

Pope, Alexander, 73

Potter, G.R., 30, 35

Principia (Newton), 73

printing press, **52**, 74, 77

  importance of, 78

  invention of, 51

Protestant Reformation, 43

Pythagoras, 42

Raphael, 11, 57, 66–67

Renaissance (1300s–1500s)

  art and, 54–67

  defining characteristics of, 10–13

  influence of classical civilizations on, 14–17

  legacy of, 68–79

republicanism, 46

Reuchlin, Johann, 49

Rivers, Isabel, 49

Roman Church, 23–25

  humanism and decline in power of, 78

  of medieval Europe, 23–25

  as patron of medieval artists, 59

  as sponsor of art, 57

Roman Empire, 16–17

  fall of, 18

Roman Forum, 17

Rousseau, Jean-Jacques, 75, 76

Russell, Jeffrey Burton, 22

Salutati, Colucci, 49

School of Athens, The (Raphael), **11**, 62, 66–67

science, 50–51

  Greek, 15–16

  humanism and, 78

  rise of, 73–74

secularism, 12, 47, 78

Ship of Fools (Brant), 12

Sider, Sandra, 38

Sistine Chapel ceiling (Michelangelo), **65**, 67

Skinner, Andrew, 51

Sophocles, 15

Tafur, Pedro, 34–35

Thompson, Bard, 62, 67

trade/trade routes, 27, 69

  exploration spurred by, 72

  Venetian/Genoese, **29**

  See also commerce

Tuchman, Barbara, 23

Turner, Jack, 29, 34

universities, 51–52

van Eyck, Hubert, 61

Venice, 30–32
Virgil, 42
Visigoths, 18

Zeckhauser, Richard, 61

Picture Credits

About the Author

Stephen Currie lives in New York State with his family. He has written books and educational materials on subjects ranging from birthdays to baseball and from ecosystems to earthquakes. He has also taught students at various grade levels from kindergarten through college.